CONCISE REFERENCE TABLE

R℞ Remedies for Writing

Kevin G. Burne, Long Beach City College

Edward H. Jones, El Camino College

Robert C. Wylder, California State College
at Long Beach

J. B. LIPPINCOTT COMPANY
Philadelphia and New York

PREFACE

This is a concise handbook of English, designed to aid the novice or the more experienced writer in solving the most frequent problems in writing and in avoiding the most frequent errors. It does not pretend to be exhaustive, but it is comprehensive enough to serve as a convenient reference. It provides a review and overview of English grammar, a discussion of the errors in grammar and usage which occur most often, and an extensive Glossary of Usage, all designed to help the writer to improve his sentences. A chapter on organizing and developing expository prose is designed to aid the writer in achieving unity and coherence in the whole essay. The index is sufficiently detailed to enable the user of the book to find what he wants quickly. The correction symbols commonly used to mark the most frequent errors are printed on the inside of the front cover along with page numbers indicating where these errors are discussed. A writer's checklist is printed on the inside of the back cover, and the "Concise Reference Table" on page i supplements the Table of Contents.

We have tried to make this book as practical and useful as possible. We hope that its brevity will contribute to its usefulness but that, despite its brevity, almost everything the average writer will need to help him write well is included within its covers. To add that little more which would change "almost everything" to "everything" would take several volumes. We are content with "almost everything," easily available.

January, 1964

K. G. B.
E. H. J.
R. C. W.

v

TABLE OF CONTENTS

LETTER TO THE READER

In preparing this book, we have assumed several things about you. You will need to know what our assumptions are if you are to get the most out of what we have included. The principal underlying assumption is that a book of essentials is what you most need. We have therefore presented what we consider to be a sound explanation of what is most important to know about grammar and composition. Besides this assumption we have made some others.

Assumption I: You do not write as well as you want to or as well as you realize you need to. Whatever the reasons for your inadequacies may be, you have become aware that the ability to write clearly is of vital importance, and you want to get to the business of improving as directly and quickly as possible. Although no book alone can make you a good writer, we think that this one, coupled with plenty of practice, can go a long way toward making you a better writer, because it concentrates on essentials and because it will help you to avoid the most frequent and troublesome errors of writing.

Assumption II: Even though you are not as competent in the use of English as you want to be, you do already know the English language well. You have been hearing and speaking and writing English all your life, having begun to learn it by ear before you were aware of the process of learning. Very early you acquired automatically the natural rhythm and word order of sentences and the beginnings of a vocabulary. By now you know most of what is basic to the structure of your language, and you know the meanings of thousands of words.

You know a good deal about English, then, and the chances are that you use it effectively most of the time. Our experience indicates that most of the errors and weaknesses in writing occur in certain rather limited areas of grammar and rhetoric, and it is upon these areas that this book concentrates. We seek to present, not an exhaustive description of written English, but only a comprehensive review of its more troublesome details and some guidelines for improvement in your writing.

Assumption III: You know some of the basic terminology and principles of grammar. Since you have had training in English at several levels, you know, at least approximately, what a noun is and what a subject is, for example. Consequently, although we have included some brief definitions

1

as review, we have tried to avoid lengthy definitions of grammatical terms which you already know. We cannot, of course, ignore terminology entirely, because it is important in talking about language.

Assumption IV: You want to start right away to learn to write English better and do not want to spend too much time on formal grammar or rules of rhetoric or fine distinctions in word choice, all of which seem secondary. We, too, want to keep the focus of this book on the process of writing, but we know from experience that the mastery of grammar and other matters which may seem like trivia is essential to learning to write well, for only when one can write correctly—can use proper capitalization, conventional spelling, standard punctuation, and sound sentences—can he turn his attention wholly to the larger problems of composition like overall organization and methods of paragraph development. Grammar and punctuation, for example, are only means to the end of good writing, but they may not be neglected. This book deals with both the means and the ends as inseparable parts of the whole process of writing well.

Assumption V: You have something worth writing about. Our experience leads us to believe that most people have interesting and even exciting things to say and that they can begin saying them right away, developing skills in expression as they go along. You have friends, associations, ideas, experiences of all kinds, and you have been collecting miscellaneous information from your reading for years. Undoubtedly you will have very little trouble in finding something to write about.

Assumption VI: You want to learn to write well and are willing to work hard to do so. If this assumption is wrong, we cannot help you very much, for writing well is not easy: there are no shortcuts to excellence. But if this assumption is right, you have every chance of success.

Chapter I

BACKGROUND FACTS AND USEFUL DISTINCTIONS

Some general information about language may prove useful by providing a perspective for the more detailed matters to follow.

A. What is a language? A language is a system of arbitrary but consistently applied vocal symbols by which thought is conveyed from one human being to another. It is notable that the definition mentions vocal symbols, that is sounds, as the center of the system. We must always remember that the written language is just an invention for recording the spoken language. Writing has, of course, had a large influence upon the way our language has developed, and we normally spend more time polishing our written than our spoken English. Still, spoken English, not written English, is the living language. Latin and classical Greek are called "dead" languages because no one speaks them any longer.

"A system of . . . consistently applied vocal symbols" means simply that a meaning exists for each sound or combination of sounds we use in speaking or record in writing. Each time we use a word in a given context it means what it meant the last time we used it in the same context: the word *pencil* means a kind of writing instrument today and will mean the same thing tomorrow. Because the meaning of *pencil* continues, it becomes a fixed part of a fixed system and is passed on. Without such a system, language could not exist; unless meaning has been assigned to them, sounds are only noises and marks are only squiggles.

The process by which the meanings are assigned is largely arbitrary. This means that there is no necessary relationship between a sound and the thing or idea we have decided it will represent. The fact that each language has a different word, for instance, for the thing we call *table* is a clear indication that users of a language assign meanings to words and that the words have no intrinsic meaning of their own. The "true" meaning of a word is not something mysterious that emerges out of the nature of the thing named; the "true" name of a thing is what the namer has chosen to call it. For us today, of course, most words are already established, fixed by practice and passed on by historical process; we seldom get to play the role of namers. However, we still do have a chance now and then to provide

3

words for new things, such as a jeep, which is called that not because of any particular qualities of the machine but because someone arbitrarily assigned it that name early in World War II. *Astronaut,* a term assigned to space travelers, has been invented within the last decade or so.

The last part of our definition of language, "by which thought is conveyed from one human being to another," needs less explanation. *Thought* may be defined broadly to include facts, judgments, and emotional responses, in short the products of the thinking and feeling processes. That human beings are involved is obvious.

A language, then, is an arbitrary but relatively fixed system of words used to convey meaning. The task of any person using any language at any time is to learn the system as well as he can so that he may communicate clearly and forcefully.

B. Language changes over periods of time. Where language came from and how it got started we do not know for sure, but we do know that it has changed and continues to change. Throughout the centuries of evolution of any language, change is evident, sometimes fast, sometimes not so fast, but nevertheless continual. Even within the course of a single lifetime some appreciable changes take place, so that the language of our grandfathers may be significantly different from ours. Over a longer span of time the changes become so great that the early linguistic ancestors of a modern descendant must be considered a foreign language.

The development of English is a good example of language change. English was imported to England in the middle of the fifth century A. D. by Angles and Saxons from western Germany who overran the native Celts and submerged the Celtic language. The language of the invaders, Anglo-Saxon, influenced by Latin and by the language of Norse invaders who came later, particularly Danes, remained the language of England until the Norman Conquest. Anglo-Saxon is in many ways the basis of modern English, but it is so different that it is now taught as a foreign language.

When William the Conqueror overcame England in 1066, he brought in a new language from what is now the north of France. Although it did not replace Anglo-Saxon, it influenced Anglo-Saxon profoundly, especially the Anglo-Saxon vocabulary. To the basic stock of Anglo-Saxon words, which still are among our most frequently used words, it added Norman counterparts; for instance, Anglo-Saxon *cow* became, presumably when safely dead, Norman *beef.* Sometimes the old Anglo-Saxon word prevailed, sometimes the Norman counterpart; often both existed side by side. For the most part Anglo-Saxon grammar survived. The resulting Middle English, the language of Chaucer (*ca.* 1400) is quite different from the Anglo-

Saxon of Alfred the Great (*ca.* 900), but it is still so different from our own that we need special study to read it.

The language continued to change. Further influences coming during the Renaissance changed it gradually so that, for instance, Shakespeare's English is not that of Chaucer. However, neither is Shakespeare's that of Mark Twain, for the process of language change went on in the newer English-speaking countries as well as in England. And of course it is still going on today.

This historical development may be called "horizontal" change. At all periods of history another kind of change is also noticeable, what we might call "vertical" change. This change is the shifting of a word from one level of social usage to another or the extension of the meaning of a word through metaphor. For instance, the word *leg* was frowned upon in polite Victorian circles; *limb* was approved. Today we can say *leg* in the company of the most refined ladies and offend no one. The word has not changed in form or meaning, but it has changed in social status. By metaphoric extension, *head,* a part of the body, has come to be used to signify, among other things, the principal officer, as the *head* of a firm of contractors. Many other words have taken and are taking on new meanings by this same vertical process.

A knowledge of the history of English may seem to be of little direct practical help to anyone in writing modern English, but a realization that language changes may be quite important in establishing sensible attitudes. Anyone who assumes that language is fixed and immutable, an absolute of some kind, will usually spend more time trying to keep it "pure" than in trying to make it work. No one can stop language change. The best thing to do, then, is to understand the change and to operate harmoniously in the evolving system.

It is important, however, to recognize also that at any one time in history a language is *relatively* fixed. The process of change is slow and unpredictable. Usually no one alone can bring about much change, and everyone should therefore spend most of his effort in mastering the language as he has come to it. Only by knowing and using the language conventions of his time and place can one expect to be understood by others of his time and place.

C. Language is controlled and changed by social and cultural pressures, not by logic or law. We have no national bureaus of language purity in this country. The publishers of dictionaries and other guides to language, editors of books and newspapers, and teachers of English probably have had the most to say about what is right and wrong in language, but they have no official status as its guardians. Anyone has a right to use any word in any way he wants to; if enough people agree with his practice, he may influence the language of his time, and he can be sure he will not be arrested for sedition. For instance, *gobbledygook* is a word Maury Maverick made up to describe certain governmental jargon which sounded impressive but said little. Enough people liked it and used it that the word is now included in dictionaries. No one has declared it official, of course; there is no such thing as official English.

Furthermore, language does not necessarily conform to our ideas of logic. To cite one troublesome example, *everyone* is grammatically singular, that is it takes a singular verb and is referred to by a personal pronoun in the singular; yet it is clearly plural in implication. We say "Everyone was there" when we mean "All were there." And we would probably say "Everyone was asked to leave the room. They waited in the hall." *Everyone* takes a singular verb in the first sentence, but is referred to by a plural pronoun in the second. That is not logically consistent. Further, *ravel* and *unravel* should, one would suppose, mean rather different, perhaps opposite, things. They actually mean the same. That isn't logical, either. Neither are many other instances that might be mentioned.

Nevertheless, that is the way language works, rather by its own processes than by logic or law. If we expect it always to behave according to pre-existing patterns, we are likely to be disappointed and annoyed. The best thing to do is to study it as it exists and to use it as it comes.

D. The spoken language and the written language are in some ways alike, in some ways different. The close relationship between spoken language and written language is of course obvious. We may speak our thoughts or we may write them down without speaking them. In either case we use essentially the same vocabulary, the same grammar, the same constructions.

However, the spoken language, which we use far more than the written, has greater freedom, primarily because it can include such aids as intonation, variation of tempo, and gesture. We speak *to* someone, and if the hearer does not understand our meaning, he can ask for an explanation. Furthermore, since spoken language is employed often as a social activity more than as a thought-conveying activity, whether we are understood sometimes doesn't matter much. "How are you, Sam? How is the family?" does not really seek information as much as it assures the person addressed that the asker is friendly. Much spoken language is similarly casual.

Written language, on the other hand, is usually less casual. Because writing a word takes far more time than saying it, we can weigh each word carefully when writing. Furthermore, we are likely to resort to writing for serious communication because then we will have a record of our thoughts. Finally, because the written language cannot use intonation and gesture, it must use words with as much precision as possible; the audience is not there to question him, so the writer must be as clear as he can. For instance, a "loose living woman chaser" may be a loose living chaser of women or a chaser of loose living women. Intonation resolves the problem in the spoken language, but not in the written language. Punctuation— a loose-living woman-chaser—may help, but it cannot resolve every problem. Usually the way out is a careful choice of words in a carefully chosen order.

Spoken language and written language are very similar in most ways, then, but differ significantly because of the circumstances of their use. This book is devoted to improving written language, but much of what it has to say applies also to spoken language.

E. The purpose of written language, and the readers for whom it is intended, will determine the level of language used. In speaking, one uses different words in the locker room, the living room, and the classroom. He knows that he must use the language appropriate to the occasion. The same is true of the written language, though the range of choice is perhaps not so wide. The vocabulary and the sentence structure used will both vary according to, among other things, the age and education of the expected readers, the intention of the writer, and the complexity of the content. No formula can be devised for such matters, but they are nonetheless important. The good writer never forgets his audience. If he really means to communicate, he must do so in the language, not of himself alone, but of his readers as well. Although the audience is not so apparent to the writer as to the speaker, the writer is just as obliged as the speaker to keep his audience in mind.

The implication is clear, then: one must use the language that fits the subject, the occasion, and the level of understanding of the audience. If he does not, he is only writing words, not conveying thoughts.

F. Learning to write well involves practice and appraisal. Talking about writing and reading about it have only limited usefulness. In order to learn to write well, one must write frequently and must analyze the results to determine what went right and what went wrong. Outside help in the analysis is often beneficial, for the writer himself may not realize that what is clear to him because he wrote it may not be clear to someone else.

At any rate, the would-be writer must practice diligently and consciously. And just as a golfer needs to make slight adjustments in his swing as he practices his game, the writer must make adjustments as he practices his craft. If he does not do so, his practice will not make perfect, but only permanent.

Writing and critical appraisal, then, go hand in hand as the hopeful writer learns to make language do his bidding. The job is not an easy one, but it is possible. Almost anyone who earnestly wants to do so can learn to write adequately if he will work at it hard enough.

TERMINOLOGY

If one is to talk about the processes of writing and about the successes and failures of particular themes and essays, he should have a terminology by which discussion may be carried on economically. He should also know the distinctions between terms often used together. Most of the terms necessary for fruitful discussion are familiar from previous training. Here are a few distinctions and definitions, however, which, though familiar, may be worth emphasizing.

A. Composition and Rhetoric. A composition is an essay or theme, usually of several paragraphs. Composition is also the process by which a writer composes an essay or theme. A theme in English composition courses is typically from five to twelve paragraphs long; an essay on politics or philosophy in a journal may run from ten to three hundred pages. Both are compositions, and the process by which they were created is composition.

Rhetoric is the skill or art of composing. The term is often used interchangeably with composition—the process of composing—but perhaps implies a higher degree of artistic consciousness. It involves primarily such matters as overall organization, progression and continuity, transitions and coherence, parallel structures, variety in paragraph development, the use of repetition as a stylistic device, diction, and the use of subordination by clauses and phrases to achieve grace and precision.

B. Grammar and Usage. Grammar is the study of the forms and relationships of words within a sentence. The study of forms we call morphology. It deals mostly with the changes of form by which we indicate number in nouns (*dog-dogs*), tense in verbs (*walk-walked*), and case in personal pronouns (*he-him*). Changes in form, usually by means of suffixes, are called inflections.

The study of relationships of words within a sentence we call syntax. It deals mainly with word order (subject-verb-object) and the placement of modifiers (words, phrases, and clauses). Syntax is very important because the meaning of an English sentence depends heavily upon the order of its words. "The dog bit the man" and "The man bit the dog" are entirely different propositions.

Because order is the principal device in English for showing the relationship between words, it is possible to use various forms within given word-order patterns to convey meaning. For instance, "Her and me went to the show" is grammatical, at least to the extent that the elements of the statement come in the expected order, and the meaning is easily enough understood. "She and I went to the show" is also grammatical: it conveys the intended meaning by the expected word order. The two sentences do not use the same forms, but they do follow the same pattern.

However, in educated circles we would accept the second version as "correct" and condemn the first as "incorrect" or "illiterate." The study of the differences between what is "correct" and what is "incorrect" is the province of usage. Since we have already seen that unconventional grammar can be just as expressive as conventional, the terms "correct" and "incorrect" really imply social acceptance rather than language necessity. For instance, we say "Am I not?" rather than "Ain't I?" more because someone in the past frowned upon "Ain't I?" than because it is ungrammatical (it isn't) or illogical.

Because the choice of a level of language and of currently acceptable forms and combinations is so important, the student needs to pay more attention to usage than he does to grammar, which in large degree will take care of itself. Most of the errors students make within sentences are not in grammar but in usage. (See the Glossary of Usage and Chapter IV for many of the most frequent errors and how to avoid them.)

Usage changes, of course. In the eighteenth century, Dr. Samuel Johnson, the writer of the famous dictionary, and his illustrious circle said "You was" as a matter of course; it was "correct" to do so. Today we insist, in all but illiterate circles, on "You were." What we insist upon in language, what the current practice is at any time, is the realm of usage.

C. Mechanics. Mechanics include punctuation, capitalization, abbreviations, italics, numbers, and spelling. These are limited by some fairly rigid conventions which must be learned; the most important of these may be found in Chapter III.

D. Diction. The choice of the right word is the problem of diction. By right word we usually mean the one with the accurate denotation and the appropriate connotation. Denotation is the central meaning, the one recorded in the dictionary; connotation, the associations and overtones of the word. For instance, *female parent* and *mother* have the same denotation, but the latter carries with it overtones of affection, security, and warmth which the former lacks. *Female parent* may be appropriate terminology in sociological or biological treatises, but *mother* is more appropriate in most contexts. We do not, for instance, celebrate Female Parent's Day; we call it Mother's Day. By knowing connotations as well as denotations of words we can control the tone of our writing and appeal to the emotions as well as to the intellects of our readers.

Some diction problems arise from the fact that certain words which sound or look nearly alike may have entirely different meanings: *except-accept, moral-morale*. Confusions of this kind can be avoided by care and by the development of a large and well differentiated vocabulary. The word confusions that most often give students trouble are listed in the Glossary of Usage.

Having learned these definitions and general facts about language, the student is ready for the more specific considerations that make up the rest of this book. However, he should keep one other fact in mind: he lives in a world where language is all around him most of the time. The best way to learn the language is to be constantly aware of how it looks and how it sounds, on all levels, under all circumstances, for all purposes. We begin learning very early how to express ourselves, and we have to continue this process throughout our whole lives. Books about language will be useful tools, but the living language is in the long run the best teacher of the living language.

Chapter II

SENTENCE STRUCTURE

The almost universal distaste which students have for English classes probably stems from interminable hours of studying a subject which, for them, had little meaning and less application to their own experience. English teachers have frequently debated the value of teaching grammar, questioning whether or not a knowledge of grammar by itself produces good writing. They would agree, however, that a knowledge of grammar enables people to write better sentences. We include here, then, a section defining and giving examples of the basic grammatical elements because invariably a discussion of writing presupposes a knowledge of them and because it is only a knowledge of what a sentence is that enables a student to make his own sentences correct.

A study of grammar is necessarily a study of the sentence, for grammatical relationships are the relationships of words within a sentence.

I. THE SENTENCE

A written sentence is a group of words which are grammatically related to one another, but which are not grammatically related to what comes before or after them. It begins with a capital letter and ends with a period, question mark, or exclamation mark. A sentence is the largest grammatical unit; all other grammatical units exist within it. A person who understands the structure of a sentence and the relationships within it understands grammar.

The two most important elements in a conventional sentence are the *subject* and the *verb*.

A. Subject

The subject of a sentence names what the sentence is discussing.

S
The *boy* ran across the street.

S
In the spring the *flowers* begin to bud.

S
Freedom of speech is the right of every American citizen.

11

B. Verb

The verb of a sentence indicates what the subject is doing, what is being done to it, or that it exists.

V
Bill *threw* the ball to his brother.

V
Papers *were thrown* all over the lawn.

V
Your students *are* here.

Although the subject and the verb are the basic elements within a sentence, few sentences are so simple that they contain only these elements. The subject or the verb may have modifiers. We convey meaning, then, by these basic words; however, we do not use them in any order which whim dictates. We arrange our words in some regular pattern.

II.   WORD ORDER WITHIN THE SENTENCE

Unlike some other languages, the English language uses word order as the principal device of conveying meaning. "Boy loves girl" and "Girl loves boy" are two different considerations, even though the words involved are the same. In ninety per cent of our sentences, we use one of only four basic patterns of word order to convey meaning.

A. Subject-verb

In the subject-verb pattern, the main idea of the sentence is expressed by the subject and the verb in that order, even though there may be intervening words.

S   V
We quickly ran to our rooms.

S   V
Jeffry saw us coming around the corner.

S   V
Greg, in spite of all the noise, slept like a baby.

B. Subject-verb-object

In the subject-verb-object pattern, we must add a noun after the verb in order to convey the main idea. The object follows the verb.

S   V   O
He raised his hand.

S   V   O
During the football game, we saw a fight in the stands.

S   V   O
The boys built a tree-house in the back yard.

C. Subject-verb-indirect object-object

The third sentence pattern is formed by adding the person or thing which receives the object. This receiver, known as the *indirect object,* always appears between the verb and the object.

```
       S    V   IO              O
The student gave me his research paper.
```

```
       S     V      IO    O
Marshall wrote his wife a letter.
```

```
          S    V      IO    O
A rich widow left the church $5,000.
```

Sometimes the receiver of the object is indicated by the words *to* or *for* before the receiver. In such cases the receiver becomes the object of a preposition rather than the indirect object.

A rich widow left $5,000 *to the church.*

Ada sang *for them* an aria by Handel.

D. Subject-verb-complement

The fourth sentence pattern is formed by adding, after the verb, a *complement,* a word which either renames the subject or describes it. The verb in these sentences is known as a *linking verb,* for it links the complement with the subject. (See pp. 16, 17.) A complement which renames the subject is called a *predicate nominative.*

```
  S  V      C
Lou is the captain.
```

```
            S   V                          C
The five men brought before the judge were traitors.
```

```
 S    V     C
Ann will be president of the club next year.
```

A complement which modifies the subject is called a *predicate adjective.*

```
        S  V  C
The boy is tall.
```

```
                              S    V    C
After having walked for fifty miles, we were tired.
```

EXCEPTIONS TO BASIC SENTENCE PATTERNS

Although ninety per cent of our sentences are formed in one of the four basic patterns stated above, ten per cent follow some other pattern. The most common of these other patterns are listed below.

A. Questions

Most questions are formed by inverting the subject and the verb or part of the verb.

V S
Is Ed here?

V   S   V   O
Did you bring home a paper?

V   S   C
Is Sacramento the capital of California?

V   S   V   IO   O
Will you give Harry the money?

B. Sentences beginning with the expletives "there" and "it"

             V   S
There will be twenty people at the party.

      V   C   S
It is necessary (that he go).
(*The noun clause in parentheses is the subject.*)

C. Sentences beginning with an introductory prepositional phrase indicating place or time

             V   S
Across the street stood a little boy.

             V   S
After the storm came a period of calm.

D. Imperative sentences in which the subject (*you*) is understood

    V
Close the door.

    V
Bring the complete list of club members tomorrow.

The sentences we have been describing thus far are *simple sentences;* they contain only one subject-verb combination. Each simple sentence is an *independent clause,* a complete grammatical unit. It is possible to have two subjects or two verbs in a simple sentence as long as they form only one subject-verb combination.

      S   V
The boy ran.

      S   S   V
The boy and girl ran.

      S   S   V   V
The boy and girl ran and jumped.

In all of these examples, the subject or subjects are performing the action of the verb or verbs. The structure of the following sentence, however, is quite different.

$$
\begin{array}{cccc}
\text{S} & \text{V} & \text{S} & \text{V}
\end{array}
$$

The boy ran, and the girl jumped.

Here we have two subject-verb combinations, and instead of a simple sentence we have a *compound sentence,* a sentence formed by two independent clauses. Each clause is an independent grammatical unit, and the two clauses are joined by a coordinating conjunction, *and.* The coordinating conjunctions *and, but, for, or, nor,* and *yet* connect grammatical units of equal value. Compound sentences may contain more than two independent clauses.

An independent clause can be changed to a *dependent clause* by adding a signal of subordination: a subordinating conjunction or a relative pronoun. (See pp. 41, 42.) "The boy ran" is an independent grammatical unit, but if we place before it a signal of subordination like *when,* we have "when the boy ran," a grammatical unit which is not a sentence and therefore not an independent clause. *The dependent clause must be joined to an independent clause, for it cannot stand alone.*

The girl jumped when the boy ran.

Here we have two subject-verb combinations, but the second is part of the first; it modifies the verb of the independent clause, telling when the girl jumped. A dependent clause will always serve as a noun, an adjective, or an adverb in conjunction with an independent clause. The sentence formed by an independent clause and a dependent clause is called a *complex sentence.* A complex sentence may have more than one dependent clause.

simple sentence:	The boy knew the story. He would not tell it.
compound sentence:	The boy knew the story, but he would not tell it.
complex sentence:	Although the boy knew the story, he would not tell it.
simple sentence:	The boy is our new neighbor. He is working in his yard.
compound sentence:	The boy is our new neighbor, and he is working in his yard.
complex sentence:	The boy who is working in his yard is our new neighbor.

When a sentence contains two or more independent clauses and one or more dependent clauses, it is a *compound-complex sentence.*

Clauses and their functions are discussed more fully on pp. 33, 36, and 38.

A *phrase,* like a clause, is a group of words functioning as a grammatical unit. Unlike a clause, it does not contain a subject and a verb. It, too, may function as a noun, adjective, or adverb within an independent clause, but it may also function in these ways within a dependent clause. Phrases are discussed more fully on pp. 27, 32, 33, 35-37, and 39 under their various types: prepositional, participial, and infinitive.

III.   THE VERB

The verb, as we have seen, indicates what the subject is doing, what is being done to it, or that it exists. Verbs can be classified as *action, linking,* or *auxiliary* verbs. They change form to indicate person, number, tense, and sometimes mood. Such changes are called *inflections.*

A. Functions

1. Action verbs

A verb is an action verb if it indicates what the subject does or what happens to the subject. An action verb may be either *transitive* or *intransitive.*

a. A *transitive* verb is one which has an object or which acts upon the subject.

```
S   V   O
We saw a car.
                            S      V      O
In the middle of the room he placed a chair.
             S    V                O
The little boy threw his brother's book on the floor.
   S                           V
Money for the new building was given by the alumni association.
(Here the verb acts upon the subject.)
```

b. An *intransitive* verb is an action verb which does not have an object.

```
       S         V
The ladder was leaning against the garage.
  S    V
We talked until early in the morning.
```

2. Linking verbs

A verb is a linking verb if it is followed by a nominal (see p. 25ff.) which renames the subject or by an adjective which describes the subject. The most frequently used linking verb is the verb *to be* in its various forms: *am, is, are, was, were, shall be, will be, have been, has been, had been, shall have been, will have been.* Other linking verbs are the sensory verbs *feel, taste, look, sound, smell;* and sometimes such verbs as *appear, grow, prove,* and *turn.*

```
       S    V        C
Doris is the chairman.
```

```
       S        V                  C
Reading has been an indispensable guide to his writing.
```

```
            S     V     C
Our little boy has grown very tall.
```

```
       S                     V      C
The people on top of the cliff seemed small.
```

3. Auxiliary verbs

An auxiliary verb is a verb which gives further dimension to the main verb in its clause by changing the tense, voice, or mood, or by adding emphasis. The most common auxiliary verbs are the various forms of the verb *to be* and the following verbs:

may	could	be going to
can	would	be about to
must	should	used to
might	have	ought to
shall	has	keep
will	had	get
do	did	got

I *should* study.

We *will have been* gone an hour.

Bill *ought to* pay his dues.

I *was about to* call you on the telephone.

Garna and John *are going to get* married.

B. Inflection

Inflection refers to the changes of form by which words indicate possession, number, person, tense, and sometimes mood. Verbs change their form to indicate person, number, and tense, and they sometimes use auxiliary verbs to indicate mood and voice.

1. Person and number

The person and number (see p. 30) of a verb are determined by its subject, with which it must agree. The only inflectional ending which indicates person or number is the *s* or *es* on the third person singular form of all verbs in the present tense except *to be,* which has its own irregular inflection, and *to have,* which changes to *has.*

Person	Singular	Plural
1	I sing	We sing
2	You sing	You sing
3	He, she, it sings	They sing

2. Tense

Verbs may be inflected to indicate time. The three fundamental forms of a verb are known as its principal parts; they are the *present* or basic form, the *past,* and the *past participle.* These three forms and the *present participle* (basic form with *ing* ending) are used to make all the other forms. Most verbs form their past tenses and past participles by adding *ed, d,* or *t* to the basic form of the verb; such verbs are called *regular verbs.* Some verbs are *irregular;* that is, they form the past tense and past participle by changing the internal spelling of the basic form or even by using a different word entirely. These irregular verbs, though fewer in number than the regular ones, are much used and cause some writers a great deal of difficulty. The surest way of learning the basic parts of irregular verbs is to memorize them. Listed below are some of the most common irregular verbs.

Present	Past	Past Participle
arise	arose	arisen
awake	awoke (awaked)	awoke
bear	bore	borne
begin	began	begun
bend	bent	bent
bind	bound	bound
bite	bit	bitten
bleed	bled	bled
blow	blew	blown
break	broke	broken
breed	bred	bred
build	built	built
burst	burst	burst
buy	bought	bought
catch	caught	caught
choose	chose	chosen

Present	*Past*	*Past Participle*
cling	clung	clung
come	came	come
creep	crept	crept
deal	dealt	dealt
dig	dug	dug
dive	dived (dove)	dived
do	did	done
draw	drew	drawn
dream	dreamt (dreamed)	dreamt
drink	drank	drunk
drive	drove	driven
eat	ate	eaten
fall	fell	fallen
feed	fed	fed
fight	fought	fought
find	found	found
flee	fled	fled
fling	flung	flung
fly	flew	flown
forbid	forbade	forbidden
forget	forgot	forgotten
freeze	froze	frozen
get	got	got (gotten)
give	gave	given
go	went	gone
grind	ground	ground
grow	grew	grown
hang	hung	hung
hang	hanged	hanged (*executed*)
have	had	had
hear	heard	heard
hide	hid	hidden
hold	held	held
keep	kept	kept
kneel	knelt (kneeled)	knelt
know	knew	known
lay	laid	laid (*placed*)
lead	led	led
leap	leapt (leaped)	leapt
leave	left	left
let	let	let
lend	lent	lent
lie	lay	lain (*rested upon*)
light	lit	lit
lose	lost	lost
make	made	made

Present	Past	Past Participle
mean	meant	meant
meet	met	met
mow	mowed	mown (mowed)
pay	paid	paid
prove	proved	proved (proven)
read	read (pro. *red*)	read
ride	rode	ridden
ring	rang	rung
rise	rose	risen
run	ran	run
say	said	said
see	saw	seen
seek	sought	sought
sell	sold	sold
send	sent	sent
set	set	set
sew	sewed	sewn (sewed)
shake	shook	shaken
shave	shaved	shaven
shine	shone (shined)	shone (shined)
show	showed	shown
shoot	shot	shot
shrink	shrank	shrunk
sing	sang	sung
sink	sank	sunk
sit	sat	sat
slide	slid	slid
sling	slang	slung
sow	sowed	sowed (sown)
speak	spoke	spoken
speed	sped	sped
spin	spun	spun
spring	sprang (sprung)	sprung
stand	stood	stood
stick	stuck	stuck
sting	stung	stung
strike	struck	struck (stricken)
string	strung	strung
strive	strove (strived)	striven
swear	swore	sworn
sweep	swept	swept
swim	swam	swum
swing	swung	swung
take	took	taken
teach	taught	taught
tear	tore	torn
tell	told	told

Present	*Past*	*Past Participle*
think	thought	thought
throw	threw	thrown
wake	waked (woke)	waked (woken)
wear	wore	worn
weave	woven	woven
weep	wept	wept
win	won	won
wind	wound	wound
wring	wrung	wrung
write	wrote	written

a. *Present tense*

The present tense expresses the present time, a general truth, or a customary action. It is expressed by the basic form of the verb.

I *see* him now.

I frequently *go* to the mountains on weekends.

I *work* in a factory.

The ancients knew that the world *is* round.

Although the present time can be expressed by the basic form of the verb, we usually express it by the *present progressive form,* a form made by combining the present participle with the appropriate present form of the verb *to be.*

I *am studying* my English assignment and must stay in the library.

Allan *is washing* the car.

Who *is complaining* about a missing motor?

b. *Past tense*

The past tense expresses a time prior to the present. It is formed by adding *ed, d,* or *t* to the basic form of the verb or by changing the internal spelling.

I played, ran	We played, ran
You played, ran	You played, ran
He, she, it played, ran	They played, ran

The *past progressive tense* expresses an action continuing or in progress in past time. It is formed by adding *was* or *were* to the present participle of the verb.

I was playing	We were playing
You were playing	You were playing
He, she, or it was playing	They were playing

c. *Future tense*

The future tense expresses an action which will take place some time in the future; it is formed by adding *will* to the basic form of the verb. The use of *shall* to express future time in the first person singular and plural is slowly disappearing, as is the use of *shall* in the second and third persons to indicate determination.

I will (shall) play	We will (shall) play
You will play	You will play
He, she, it will play	They will play

Occasionally the future tense is expressed by using *going to, about to,* or *to be.*

Charles *is going to* play golf.

Mary *is about to* play her violin.

I *am to be* the next president of our club.

The *future progressive form* of the verb expresses an action which will be in progress at some future time. It is formed by adding a present participle to the future form of the verb *to be.*

I will (shall) be playing	We will (shall) be playing
You will be playing	You will be playing
He, she, it will be playing	They will be playing

d. *Perfect tenses*

The perfect tenses express either a continuing action begun in the past, an action completed at some past time, or an action to be completed at some future time.

1. *Present perfect*

    The present perfect tense, formed by adding *have* or *has* to the past participle, expresses a continuing action begun in the past.

I have played, run	We have played, run
You have played, run	You have played, run
He, she, it has played, run	They have played, run

    I have played golf for three years.

    He has studied all week for this examination.

2. *Past perfect*

    The past perfect tense, formed by adding *had* to the past

participle, expresses an action completed by some stated or implied time in the past.

I had played	We had played
You had played	You had played
He, she, it had played	They had played

Greg broke the kite that he had made.

Jane had read the book before she saw the picture.

3. *Future perfect*

The future perfect tense, formed by adding *will have* to the past participle, expresses an action to be completed by some future time.

I will (shall) have played	We will (shall) have played
You will have played	You will have played
He, she, it will have played	They will have played

By tomorrow morning I will have finished the book.

In June, Joe will have been working here ten years.

As with the present, past, and future tenses, the perfect tenses may be expressed in the progressive forms.

Allen *has been going* to college for three years.

Betty and the committee *had been meeting* on Thursday afternoons before vacation began.

When we reach Kansas City, we *will have been driving* for three hours.

The following chart may be helpful in indicating the relationship of the various tenses.

Past	Present	Future
I played golf.	I play golf. I am playing golf.	I will play golf.
I have played golf. Present perfect (*have, has*)		
I had played golf. Past perfect (*had*)		I will have played golf. Future perfect (*will have shall have*)

Present perfect—continuing action begun in the past.

Past perfect—action completed at some indicated past time.

Future perfect—action completed at some indicated future time.

3. Mood

Mood is that quality of the verb which indicates the manner in which a verb is expressed. There are three moods: *indicative, subjunctive,* and *imperative.*

a. *Indicative mood*
   The indicative mood is used to make a statement or to ask a question. This is by far the most used of the three moods.

   Your library book is overdue.

   Smith committed two errors in the ninth inning.

   Where are you going?

b. *Subjunctive mood*
   The subjunctive mood, one that has all but disappeared in modern usage, expresses a wish, a doubt, or a statement contrary to fact. It is formed by changing the indicative *was* to *were.* The subjunctive is also used in legal documents, parliamentary procedure, and clauses of necessity.

   I wish I were a millionaire.

   Bill would help you if he were not so busy.

   We believe it necessary that he attend the meeting.

   I move that the meeting be adjourned.

c. *Imperative mood*
   The imperative mood expresses a command or request. It seldom is used with a subject, and it is always expressed by the basic form of the verb.

   Close the door.

   Pick up your papers in my office.

4. Voice

The voice of a verb indicates whether the subject acts or is acted upon. A verb is in either the *active* or *passive* voice.

a. *Active voice*
   A verb is in the active voice when its subject is the performer of the action.

   Our class *will hold* its reunion on April 22.

   We *gathered* the firewood just outside the campground.

b. *Passive voice*

A verb is in the passive voice when its subject is the receiver of the action, in which case the verb, instead of denoting an action performed by the subject, denotes an action performed to or on the subject. The passive voice is formed by combining some form of the verb *to be* with the past participle of a transitive verb.

Our class reunion *will be held* on April 22.

The firewood *was gathered* just outside the campground.

5. Emphasis

The emphatic form of the verb strengthens an assertion. It consists of a verb preceded by the appropriate form of the verb *to do*. The verb *to do* is also used to form questions which can be answered with "yes" or "no."

I *do play* the piano.

Do you think that taxes will be raised next year?

Bill *did attend* the meeting last month.

6. Compounded verbs

Some verbs are formed by adding to a verb a word which usually functions as a preposition.

We *turned on* our flashlights when we went into the cave.

The boy *blew up* the balloon, and the balloon blew up the chimney.

IV. THE NOMINAL

A nominal word is any word, phrase, or clause which names something: a person, place, thing, quality, or idea. Nominals can be classified by their function (subject, object, indirect object, predicate nominative, object of the preposition, nominal of address, or appositive) or by their type (noun, pronoun, participle, infinitive, or clause).

A. Functions of nominals

As we have seen in section II, we usually express ourselves in one of four basic sentence patterns, which, in addition to the subject and the verb, may contain an object, indirect object, predicate nominative, or predicate adjective. Each of these elements, except for the predicate adjective, is a *nominal.* In addition to these, a nominal may name the object of a preposition or a person whom we are addressing (nominal of address), or it may merely rename some other nominal within the sentence (appositive). The following are examples of each of these nominal functions.

1. Subject

The subject is the nominal which names whoever or whatever the sentence is about, except in imperative sentences, in which the subject is usually implied.

My *wife* bought a new dress.

She spent too much money.

Buying dresses is her hobby.

What she spent did not surprise me.

2. Object

The object is the nominal which names the receiver of the action of the verb, even though that action may be minimal.

Mary caught the *ball.*

I have a *book.*

She surprised *me.*

Leslie likes *to play the cello.*

She did not remember *how she did it.*

3. Indirect object

The indirect object is the nominal which names the receiver of the object.

Throckmorton wrote *Ed* a letter.

Ed had already sent *him* a check.

Both of them had given the *college* their annual contribution.

4. Predicate nominative

The predicate nominative renames the subject of its clause and is joined to it by a linking verb.

Henry is the *chairman.*

His favorite sport is *skiing.*

He was always the first *one* to finish his work.

He became *chairman* last year.

5. Object of the preposition

The object of the preposition is the nominal which follows the preposition. The preposition and its object and modifiers form a phrase which functions as a modifier.

Four boys raced (around the *corner*).

One (of *them*) fell.

They paid no attention (to *what I said*).

6. Nominal of address

The nominal of address is a nominal used for the purpose of speaking or writing directly to someone.

Bill, your car is parked near a fire plug.

Why didn't you move it, *Jane?*

Sir, you should move it yourself.

Will you, *Mr. Johnson,* move it for me?

7. Appositive

The appositive is a nominal which restates another nominal with no intervening verb.

Our teacher, *Miss Fitzhugh,* requires us to write a research paper.

Writing papers, a *job* which I dislike, is a necessary evil in every English class.

My brother *Bob* likes to write.

B. Types of nominals

In addition to being classified by their function, nominals may also be classified by the way they perform their naming function, that is, as nouns, pronouns, participles, infinitives, phrases, or clauses.

1. Nouns

A noun is a word which names someone or something. It may or may not be identified by a noun indicator (*a, an, the,* or a possessive), which, when present, appears immediately before a noun or before the adjective which modifies a noun. A noun may also be identified by the manner in which it is inflected:

it may add *s* or *es* or change its spelling to form the plural, or it may add *'s* or merely *'* to form the possessive.

The *girl* waved to the *engineer.*

Exercise builds strong *muscles.*

Bill's *ideas* are worth *consideration.*

The *sermon* dealt with the *necessity* for *tolerance.*

a. *Noun types*

The three types of nouns are common, proper, and collective.

1. *Common and proper nouns*

A common noun designates a class of persons, places, or things. A proper noun designates a particular member of a class. Hence *boy* is a common noun, for there are many persons included in the class labeled *boy. John* is a proper noun, for it names a particular boy. Proper nouns are always capitalized.

Common	Proper
school	Yale University
building	Empire State Building
bridge	Brooklyn Bridge
city	Long Beach
history	History 33
aunt	Aunt Beverly

2. *Collective nouns*

A collective noun designates a group rather than an object or individual. Collective nouns may be either singular or plural, depending on whether they designate the group or the individuals within the group. Examples are *army, jury, committee, troop, team, class, audience.* (See p. 56.)

b. *Noun inflections*

Nouns are inflected to indicate number (whether they are singular or plural) or to indicate possession.

1. *Number*

Nouns may be either singular (denoting one) or plural (denoting more than one). A singular noun is made plural by adding *s (boy, boys)* or *es (potato, potatoes),* or by changing one or more vowels within the word *(man, men; goose, geese*). A few nouns form their plurals by adding *en* (*child, children*). Some nouns have the same form in the singular and the plural (*sheep, deer*). When non-hyphenated compound nouns are made plural, the last part usually takes the plural form (*tablecloth, tablecloths; teaspoon, teaspoons;* but *brother-in-law, brothers-in-law*).

2. *Possessives*

Nouns may be inflected to denote ownership or a similar close relationship. A possessive is formed by adding *'s* to a noun or, if the noun ends with an *s*, merely by adding an apostrophe. It is important to remember that whatever comes before the apostrophe is the noun as it stood before it was made possessive.

A noun which has been made possessive becomes a noun indicator rather than a nominal because it no longer has a naming function.

boy	boy's
boys	boys'
John	John's
children	children's
Keats	Keats' or Keats's
Jones	Jones' or Jones's
Kresses	Kresses'

2. Pronouns

A pronoun is a word which refers to and derives its meaning from an already stated noun or pronoun (except for the indefinite pronouns and *I, you, we, me,* and *us*). The noun or pronoun to which a pronoun refers is its *antecedent.*

Every boy should say whether or not *he* has finished *his* work.

She said *she* had finished her work.

The major types of pronouns are the *personal, indefinite, demonstrative, relative, interrogative, reflexive,* and *intensive.*

a. *Personal pronouns*

Personal pronouns are so called because they are the only pronouns which have different forms to indicate person. They also have special forms to indicate number, gender, and case.

1. *Person*

   Grammatical person means that the person represented by the pronoun indicates the speaker (first person), the one spoken to (second person), or the one spoken about (third person). (See chart below.)

2. *Number*

   Pronouns are either singular, referring to one, or plural, referring to more than one. A singular pronoun refers to a singular antecedent, a plural pronoun to a plural antecedent.

3. *Gender*

   Personal pronouns in the third person singular have different forms for masculine (*he*), feminine (*she*), and neuter (*it*). Each must refer to its appropriate antecedent.

4. *Case*

   Case means changes in form which indicate whether the pronoun is functioning as a subject or predicate noun (subjective case), object (objective case), or possessive (possessive case).

CHART OF PERSONAL PRONOUNS

Person	Case					
	Subjective		Objective		Possessive	
	singular	plural	singular	plural	singular	plural
First	*I*	*we*	*me*	*us*	*my, mine*	*our, ours*
Second	*you*	*you*	*you*	*you*	*your, yours*	*your, yours*
Third	m. *he*	*they*	*him*	*them*	*his, his*	*their, theirs*
	f. *she*		*her*		*her, hers*	
	n. *it*		*it*		*its, its*	
	who (relative pro)		*whom* (relative pro)		*whose* (relative pro)	

Note: Possessive pronouns, except *mine, yours, hers, its, ours* and *theirs,* function as adjectivals rather than nominals.

b. *Indefinite pronouns* SINGULAR

Indefinite pronouns are similar to nouns in that they do not depend on antecedents. Because they indicate groups or collections rather than specific antecedents, they are sometimes called *indefinite nouns.* They can be divided into two groups: those which have a possessive form (group I) and those which do not (group II).

I.	anybody	somebody	everybody	nobody	neither
	anyone	someone	everyone	no one	either
				one	another
				other	the other
II.	any	some	each	nothing	
	anything	something	everything		
	all	few		none	
	many	several			

c. *Demonstrative pronouns*

A demonstrative pronoun points out with particular emphasis a person, place, or thing. The four demonstrative pronouns are *this* and *that* (singular) and *these* and *those* (plural). These words are pronouns only when they stand alone, for when one of them precedes a noun (*this book, those girls*) it becomes an adjective.

This is mine.

I was not referring to *that.*

Those are Bob's golf clubs.

d. *Relative pronouns*

A relative pronoun (*who, whom, which, that, whose*) connects a dependent clause to an independent clause. Of these pronouns, *who* is subjective, *whom* objective, and *whose* possessive. The case of a relative pronoun is determined by its function in the dependent clause (see p. 15), not by its antecedent.

Mr. Caldwell knows the one *who* will describe your job.

This chapter is one *which* you will have to read with care.

Here is a problem *that* will give you little trouble.

e. *Interrogative pronouns*

The interrogative pronouns (*who, whom, whose, which, what*) ask questions which demand more than a yes or no response.

Unlike interrogative adverbs (*where, when, how, why*), interrogative pronouns function only as nominals. *Whose, which,*
and *what* are pronouns only when they stand alone, for when
one of them precedes a noun (*whose book, which play, what
night*) it becomes an adjective.

Who broke the window?

What did you say?

Whose is it?

f. *Reflexive pronouns*

A reflexive pronoun, always the object of a verb or a preposition, refers to the subject of its construction. It consists of
the personal pronoun with the suffix *self* or *selves*. The
following are reflexive pronouns.

myself	ourselves
yourself	yourselves
himself, herself, itself	themselves

(There are no such words as *hisself* and *theirselves*.)

Did you hurt *yourself?*

We let the children look out for *themselves*.

g. *Intensive pronouns*

An intensive pronoun has the same form as a reflexive pronoun, but it emphasizes and is in apposition with its antecedent.

I will do the work *myself*.

The president *himself* was there.

Mary Jones *herself* did all of the typing.

3. **Participle**   ING ᴇPRECEDING VERB USE POSSESSIVE

A present participle (ending in *ing*) is a nominal when it names
an act. It may also function as a part of the verb or as an adjectival, but it is only the nominal function which concerns us here.
(The participle used as a nominal is frequently called a *gerund*.)

Hiking is fun.

Miss Bergman is well known for her *acting*.

Even though a participle functions as a nominal, it is still a verb form and can have an object or a complement or be modified. A participle may also have tense, which can be indicated by an auxiliary verb, in which case the auxiliary verb takes the *ing* ending.

A participle, with any object, any complement, or any adverbial it may take, forms a *participial phrase.* The whole phrase, then, constitutes a single grammatical unit, in this case a nominal.

Walking through the graveyard was an exhilarating exercise.

My greatest surprise was *being named on the Dean's list.*

4. Infinitives

An infinitive is a construction made up of the basic form of the verb usually preceded by *to.* Infinitives may function as nominals, adverbials, or adjectivals. However, it is only the nominal function which concerns us here.

Laura wanted *to sing.*

Our aim is *to win.*

To relax is *to enjoy* good health.

He helped me *work.*

Like the participle, the infinitive may have adverbial modifiers, an object, or a complement, thus forming an *infinitive phrase.* An infinitive may also change its form by auxiliary verbs.

John asked *to see his paper.*

To get a campsite was almost impossible.

The judge told the defendant *to pay his fine.*

It is not like him *to have forgotten the tickets.*

The construction formed by an infinitive or an infinitive phrase preceded by a noun or a pronoun in the objective case is a special construction, a kind of clause equivalent.

The officer asked *us to wait.*

The senior class wanted *Mr. Smith to be the graduation speaker.*

5. Noun clause

A noun clause is a dependent clause which functions as a nominal. The connectives which usually introduce noun clauses are *who, whom, whoever, whomever, which, that, what, whatever, when, why, how, whether.*

What you said surprised me.

I asked him *how he enjoyed his vacation.*

The guard will be *whomever I choose.*

Occasionally the connecting word may be omitted.

He said *he would be late.*

Jeffry knew *he would not be able to go.*

V. THE MODIFIER

Although the basic idea of a sentence is expressed by the subject, verb, and whatever objects or complements the verb may have, these elements alone do not usually express our precise meaning. *Modifiers* are necessary to sharpen the general meaning. Modifiers are those elements which make the meaning of nominals and verbs more specific by describing, qualifying, or limiting.

Modifiers are classified by their function and by their type. Although modifiers have several functions, they fall into two major types: those which modify nominals, and those which modify verbs and other modifiers.

A. Nominal modifiers—adjectivals

An adjectival is a word, phrase, or clause which modifies a nominal. It may be an adjective, participle, infinitive, phrase, or clause.

1. Adjective

An adjective is a single word which modifies a nominal. Its position in a sentence is relatively fixed, for it usually precedes the noun it modifies, or, in the case of the predicate adjective, appears after a linking verb and modifies the subject. Occasionally it appears after the noun it modifies, but in such cases it is usually set apart by commas.

The blue car sped down   the dark street.
Everyone was silent after the dull speech.
Richard Cory, despondent and weary, killed himself.

a. *Proper adjectives*

A proper adjective is an adjective derived from a proper noun. It is always capitalized.

America	American
China	Chinese
Congress	Congressional
Freud	Freudian

b. *Interrogative adjectives*

An interrogative adjective (*which, what, whose, how many*) is used to form a question. An interrogative adjective always modifies an expressed nominal.

Which house is yours?

What time does the dance begin?

2. Participles

Both the present (*ing* ending) and the past participle (*d, ed, t, en,* or *n* ending or change of basic verb form) may function as an adjectival. Auxiliary forms may change the tense or voice of participles.

We heard the clock *ticking.*

Growling, the dog approached the little boy.

The *broken* toys lay all over the floor.

The little girl, *having fallen,* cried as she ran home.

A participle, with any object, complement, or modifier it may have, forms a participial phrase, which may function as an adjectival.

Charles, *throwing his putter against a tree,* stalked toward the clubhouse.

Having prepared very well, I was not worried about the examination.

The old man *arrested by the police* claimed he was innocent.

3. Infinitives

An infinitive or an infinitive phrase, which we have seen function as a nominal, may also function as an adjectival.

This is a good place *to study.*

The chapters *to read* for tomorrow's lecture are listed on the board.

4. Prepositional phrases

A prepositional phrase functions as an adjectival when it modifies a nominal.

These books *on the desk* are yours.
Mrs. Jackson lives in the house *across the street.*

5. Clauses

A clause is an adjectival when it modifies a nominal. The words which most frequently introduce adjective clauses are the relative pronouns *who, whom, whose, which, that* and in special cases the relative adverbs *where, when, before, after.* Almost invariably, the adjective clause follows immediately after the word it modifies.

He is the man *who will help you.*
We returned to the place *where he had left his wallet.*
Tom will arrive in Los Angeles three hours *after he leaves Chicago.*

In some cases the introductory word may be omitted from an adjective clause.

We sold the car *you were asking about.*
The job *Mr. Kingsbury wanted* is no longer available.

B. Verb modifiers and modifiers of other elements—adverbials

An adverbial is a word, phrase, or clause which modifies a verb or another modifier. It may be an adverb, an infinitive, a phrase, or a clause.

1. Adverb

An adverb is a single word whose typical function is to modify a verb or another modifier. It indicates time, place, manner, degree, direction, or frequency and answers the questions *when, where, why, how much,* or *how.* The position of an adverb is not so fixed as the position of an adjective.

The children walked *slowly* to school.

Our club is having a picnic *tomorrow.*

Tomorrow our club is having a picnic.

Who is taking you *home?*

I am *exceedingly* wealthy.

Many adverbs are formed by adding *-ly* to an adjective *(bad-badly, quick-quickly, glad-gladly)*; however, not all words ending in *-ly* are adverbs. For instance, some adjectives are formed by adding *-ly* to a noun *(time-timely, man-manly, friend-friendly).* Interrogative adverbs *(where, when, why, how)* are used in asking questions.

Where are you going?

When is the meeting to be held?

2. Infinitives

An infinitive or an infinitive phrase functions as an adverb when it modifies a verb, adjective, or adverb.

She went to the library *to study.*

He is too young *to go.*

Doris went to New York *to see her mother.*

My son said he was ready *to take the driving test.*

3. Prepositional phrases

A prepositional phrase functions as an adverbial when it modifies a verb.

We will meet you *at the Sports Arena.*

Beside the house stood an old tree.

4. Clauses

A clause functions as an adverbial when it modifies a verb or a modifier. Adverbial clauses may be classified by what they indicate: place, time, cause, concession, purpose, manner, result, condition, comparison, or degree. Adverbial clauses are introduced by subordinating conjunctions.

The following examples illustrate the various kinds of adverbial clauses with most of the subordinating conjunctions which introduce them.

Place:	where, wherever I will go *wherever you go.*
Time:	since, while, when, whenever, after, before, as *While you were at lunch,* Mr. Brouwers called.
Manner:	as, as if, as though Mrs. Hamel sang the song *as it was written.*
Cause:	because, inasmuch as, since Bill came home early *because he ran out of money.*
Concession:	though, although, even if *Although we had spent hours in preparation,* we were not ready.
Purpose:	that, so that, in order that Ned stood *so that I could have his seat.*
Result:	so that, so The cloud covered the moon *so that the night became darker still.*
Condition:	if, provided that, in case, in case that *If you can get there early,* you can get a good seat.
Comparison:	than, as . . . as, so . . . as Harold paints *as* well *as his brother.*
Degree:	than, as . . . as, so . . . that It was *so* warm *that I took my sweater off.*

C. Comparison of modifiers

Both adverbs and adjectives may have an *er* or *est* ending, may be preceded by *more* or *most,* or may change form to indicate comparison. The comparative degree (the *er* ending or the word preceded by *more*) is used to compare two nominals or two verbs; the superlative degree (*est* ending or the word preceded by *most*) is used to compare three or more nominals or three verbs. *More* or *most* are usually used with adjectives or adverbs having three or more syllables. *Less* and *least* are used to indicate a degree lower than the positive degree. Some adjectives cannot be compared (*round, square, unique, secret, perfect*) because they express ultimates in themselves: there is no degree of roundness or of perfection.

Gregory is the *shorter* of the two boys.

Matilda is the *most beautiful* girl in the office.

Our 440 man is running *slower* this year.

The *oldest* man there performed *best* of all.

This is the *least serious* of all my worries.

The workmen are earning *less* money than they expected.

VI. STRUCTURE WORDS

Structure words are those words which combine the basic elements of a sentence—nominals, verbs, adverbials, and adjectivals—into meaningful sentences. They are classified according to their function as prepositions, connectives, expletives, or noun indicators.

A. Prepositions

A preposition is a word which expresses a relationship between two nominals; it usually introduces a group of words, one of which must be the object of a preposition, a nominal. This group of words, including the preposition, the object, and any modifiers it may have, is a prepositional phrase. The phrase as a whole functions as an adverbial or an adjectival. (See pp. 34, 36, 37.)

We walked *across the street*. (adverbial)

The house *across the street* has been vacant for weeks. (adjectival)

Laurie will not meet you *on the corner*. (adverbial)

Jane is going to the store *on the corner*. (adjectival)

The most commonly used prepositions are listed below. (Some of these words function also as subordinating conjunctions and as adverbs.)

about	according to	ahead of	apart from
above	after	along	around
across	against	among	as

as far as	despite	near	through
as for	down	of	throughout
as to	during	off	till
at	except	on	to
back of	excepting	on account of	toward
because of	for	onto	towards
before	from	out	under
behind	in	out of	underneath
below	in addition to	outside	until
beneath	in back of	outside of	unto
beside	in place of	over	up
between	instead of	owing to	up to
beyond	in spite of	past	upon
but (except)	in view of	rather than	with
by	inside	regarding	within
concerning	into	round	without
contrary to	like	since	

B. Connectives

A connective joins words, phrases, clauses, sentences, or even paragraphs. The connectives are coordinating conjunctions, subordinating conjunctions, relative pronouns, and transitional words.

1. Coordinating conjunctions

A coordinating conjunction connects elements of similar grammatical form within a sentence. The common coordinating conjunctions are *and, but, for, or, nor,* and *yet.* (*For* is a coordinating
conjunction only between independent clauses. *Yet* is sometimes
considered a transition word.)

Ben *and* George play golf rather poorly.

The students can study *or* read in the library.

Marshall had to attend the meeting, *for* he was the chairman of the committee.

The team played its best, *but* we still lost the game.

Don was working quickly *yet* neatly.

Some coordinating conjunctions, called *correlative conjunctions,* work in pairs. The chief correlative conjunctions are

both . . . and	either . . . or
not only . . . but also	neither . . . nor

Both adults *and* children are welcome.

You may write with *either* pen *or* pencil.

We want *not only* your attention *but also* your interest.

2. Subordinating conjunctions

A subordinating conjunction introduces a dependent clause, either noun or adverb, and connects it to another clause. The dependent clause has its own subject and verb but cannot stand alone as a sentence. (Clauses are discussed more fully under their types: see nominal, adjectival, adverbial.) Some typical subordinating conjunctions are

after	before	provided that	unless
although	even if	since	until
as	even though	so that	when
as . . . as	if	so . . . that	whenever
as if	in case	so . . . as	where
as though	in case that	than	wherever
because	in order that	that	while
	inasmuch as	though	

Harry waved his cigar in the air *while* he talked.

He looked *as though* he had not eaten for days.

Please do not borrow the book *unless* you can return it before Monday.

Ned is *as* tall *as* Greg.

3. Relative pronouns

A relative pronoun connects an adjective clause to another clause, or it introduces a noun clause. It functions as a nominal within its own clause, except for *whose,* which is a possessive. The relative pronouns are

who	which
whom	that
whose	

Who and *whom* refer to people, *which* refers to things, and *that* refers to people or things.

David is the one *who* holds the school record in the high hurdles. (*adj.*)

Chris saw the girl *whom* we wanted to meet. (*adj.*)

This is one of the scenes *which* we will always remember. (*adj.*)

He is a man *whose* word is his bond. (*adj.*)

That you were out last night is no excuse for not completing your work. (*noun*)

Dr. Booth knows *whom* you must see. (*noun*)

4. Transition words

A transitional word relates one independent clause, one sentence, or one paragraph to another. Usually a transitional word comes at the beginning of the second clause, sentence, or paragraph, but, unlike a subordinating conjunction, it may be placed elsewhere within a clause. The most common transitional words are *however, therefore, furthermore, meanwhile, otherwise, nevertheless, consequently, moreover, yet, accordingly, also, anyhow, besides, hence, indeed, instead, likewise, still, then, thus;* and such transitional phrases as *for example, in fact, in other words, on the contrary, on the other hand,* and *that is.*

Mr. Brewer said that he would not serve as treasurer next year; *therefore,* we will have to appoint someone else.

I was unable to preregister for classes last spring; *consequently,* many of the classes I wanted were closed.

Nancy must practice her piano lesson; she may, *however,* do her arithmetic first.

C. Noun indicators

A noun indicator is a word which signals that a noun or a participle is to follow. The only word which can separate a noun indicator from the noun which follows it is an adjective. The noun indicators are the articles (*a, an, the*) and the possessives, both noun and pronoun. The definite article *the* points out a more specific noun than do the indefinite articles *a* and *an.* (See Glossary of Usage.)

A man stopped by to see you.

Doris said that she had read *the* book.

My old house was sold last week.

We went to the game in *Dick's* car.

D. Expletives

An expletive is a special word which introduces a sentence but has no other grammatical or content value. The expletives are *there* and *it*. Neither is the subject; the subject comes after the verb. (*There* is also used as an adverb.)

There were five people in the room.

There was no reason for his being so late.

It is important that you remember your part.

It is necessary to go early.

VII. THE ABSOLUTE CONSTRUCTION

An absolute construction is a sentence modifier rather than a modifier of any particular element within the sentence. It is frequently adverbial by implication, for it can be replaced by an adverbial clause. An absolute phrase is formed by a noun or pronoun followed by a participle, a prepositional phrase, or an adjective.   AVOID   BEING

The day being cloudy, we decided to stay home.

The men started to get restless, *their work being almost completed.*

My mother, *flour all over her apron,* looked up and smiled.

Chapter III

PUNCTUATION AND MECHANICS

Punctuation marks are readers' marks, for they help make written communication clear by indicating grammatical relationships. A recognition of the functions of these marks is of utmost importance to the person who wishes to write clearly, for the careful writer does not use punctuation marks indiscriminately.

Punctuation is a matter of convention. People have agreed that certain marks indicate certain grammatical relationships. The period, question mark, and exclamation mark indicate the end of sentences; the colon, semicolon, comma, and dash indicate breaks within sentences; the hyphen indicates a break within a word or a joining of words expressing one idea; the indention of a paragraph indicates a break between two groups of sentences which develop different ideas; and quotation marks, italics, and brackets have other special functions. It is important to remember that all of these marks join or separate grammatical units and that correct punctuation depends upon a knowledge of these units.

I. END PUNCTUATION—PERIOD, QUESTION MARK, EXCLAMATION MARK

A period is used to mark the end of a declarative or an imperative sentence. A question mark is used at the end of an interrogative sentence, and an exclamation mark is used at the end of an exclamatory sentence.

He left early so that he could get a ticket for the show.

Please put the book on the table.

What time is it?

Get out!

Period

1. A period is used at the end of a declarative sentence even if the sentence consists of only one word.

   The car is parked in the driveway.

   "Have you seen the new Fords yet?" he asked.

   "No."

2. A period is used after an abbreviation except in the case of well-known national or international agencies. (Consult a reliable dictionary for forms of abbreviations.)

Jacob Harrington, M.D., gave the opening address.

His office is on the sixth floor of the UN building.

Mr. Smith stopped by Miss Thompson's office.

3. A period is used after a number or letter in an outline.

I. Sources of the library

   A. Card catalog

   B. Periodical room

      1. *Reader's Guide*

      2. *International Index*

Question mark

A question mark is used with a direct question. It falls inside the quotation marks if it is part of a quotation, outside if it is not.

He asked, "Where are you going?"

Who said, "Don't do that"?

Who asked, "What time is it?"

"Are you going?" she asked.

Notice that an indirect question is declarative and not interrogative; therefore, it takes a period.

He asked me how I was.

He wondered if you could go.

Exclamation mark

An exclamation mark *may* be used after an exclamatory word, phrase, clause or sentence.

Oh!

What a day!

Get out of the way!

II. SEMICOLON

1. A semicolon is used to separate two closely related independent clauses when no coordinating conjunction is used.

John left the party at midnight; we left shortly afterwards.

2. A semicolon is used between two independent clauses joined by a transitional word (*however, moreover, nevertheless, consequently, still, therefore, thus, furthermore, meanwhile, otherwise, yet,* etc.,) or by such introductory words as *namely, for example, for instance, that is,* when they introduce a second independent clause.

We were unable to attend the opening of the play; consequently, we gave our tickets away.

He would not do the required work; moreover, he would not let anyone else do it.

He is a real craftsman; for example, he built this cabinet.

He was a poor student; in the first place, he had trouble reading.

3. A semicolon is used to separate items in a series when commas are used within the items.

The fruit stand displayed apples, big and red; oranges, round and juicy looking; and grapes, both red and purple.

The shipment of radios was routed through San Francisco, California; Reno, Nevada; and Salt Lake City, Utah.

III. COLON

1. A colon means *namely,* and it points to a restatement, explanation, or a list which is to follow. It is important to remember that in formal writing a complete sentence must precede a colon. A colon is not used immediately after verbs or after *such as.*

He brought the following items: a wrench, a saw, and some pliers.

The conclusion was clear: he was a thief.

2. A colon is frequently used to introduce a formal question.

The question before the committee is this: what can we do to raise funds?

3. A colon is used to emphasize an appositive.

He had one thing on his mind all the time: boats.

4. A colon also is used between the act and the scene of a play, the hour and minute denoting time, chapter and verse in the Bible; after the salutation in a business letter; in mathematical ratios; and in certain elliptical constructions.

Hamlet V:1
7:03 p.m.
Luke 11:20
Dear Sir:
4:8::1:2
Conclusion:

IV. COMMA

Actually there are only four general uses of the comma:

A. To separate independent clauses when a coordinate conjunction (*and, but, or, for, nor, yet*) is used.

We drove to the station, and Jim filled the tank with gasoline.

If the independent clauses are short and closely related, the comma may be omitted.

He stayed but we left early.

B. To separate words or groups of words in a coordinate series, including the last two items.

They brought apples, oranges, and pears.

We fished in the lake, in the stream, and in the river.

We wondered how it was built, when it was built, and where it was built.

A comma is used between coordinate adjectives, that is, adjectives in a series that modify a noun in the same manner.

As we walked down the path, we saw a narrow, winding road far ahead.

A furious, screaming old woman yelled at the wrestler.

C. To separate introductory clauses and phrases from the rest of the sentence.

If I have time, I shall do it. (adverb clause)

In the very densely populated areas, transportation is good. (long prepositional phrase)

Climbing the mountain, we were able to see the distant ocean. (participle phrase)

D. To set off parenthetic elements.

1. To set off an absolute construction from the rest of the sentence.

    The rain having stopped, we left.

    The forces landed, the night being very dark, without the loss of a man.

2. To set off transitional words such as *however, moreover, nevertheless, consequently,* and *thus* and such introductory phrases as *in the first place* and *on the other hand.*

    He could not, however, get the work finished.

    Frank did the work; consequently, it was done right.

    John could not do the painting; on the other hand, his friend could do it very well.

It may be said that the trend is away from using commas with transition words preceded by coordinating conjunctions.

He arrived early, and consequently he had a good view of the game.

3. To set off words or phrases out of their usual order.

The old man, weary and discouraged, sat down with a sigh.

The mountains, purple in the distance, were very high.

4. To set off interjections.

Well, what shall we do?

No, I cannot help you.

5. To set off contrasted coordinate **elements.**

I will do the sewing, not you.

Ralph, not Bill, will be able to get the information.

6. To set off a noun in direct address.

Peggy, let's go to the beach.

What do you, John, think about the question?

7. To set off non-restrictive elements. A non-restrictive element is a grammatical unit which adds information to a noun or pronoun already clearly identified within a sentence.

Roger, who was spokesman for the group, requested more information.

Harding's first book, which he wrote at the age of twenty, was very exciting reading.

Mr. Stillson, our regular mailman, did not bring the letter.

One of my friends, Thompson, helped me fix the car.

The mechanic who usually fixes your car is away on vacation. (*Restrictive adjective clauses use no commas.*)

8. To set off a direct quotation in a sentence.

He said, "I will not go."

In the opposite stand could be heard the cry, "Hold that line!"

"I see what you mean," was all he would say.

"I don't know," said George, "if we can get there on time."

9. To set off a parenthetic expression.

He was not, in my opinion, able to do the work.

Victor Telleson, Ph.D., will speak tonight.

10. To set off elements after the first one in dates and addresses.

> He was born on July 10, 1922, in Virginia.

> My friend lives at 715 Manhattan Avenue, Carby Beach, Florida.

11. To prevent misreading.

> Inside, the dog was chewing on the bone.

> After washing, Margaret prepared dinner.

> After washing Judy, we prepared dinner.

V.   QUOTATION MARKS

A direct quotation is enclosed in quotation marks.

> He said, "We will be there at 5:00 o'clock."

In a quotation consisting of several paragraphs, quotation marks are placed at the beginning of each paragraph, but at the end of only the last.

Quotation marks enclose names of essays, short stories, chapters, short poems, and articles; indicate a word being discussed; and set off a word or expression which is more formal or less formal than the context of the passage.

> "Where are you going?" John asked.

> "I'll be there," he said.

> Who said, "I am not going"?

> He read Keats' "Lamia."

> She couldn't spell the word "vacuum."

> The foreman said that he was "bushed."

VI.   DASH

Dashes set off parenthetic material which the writer wishes to emphasize within a sentence. The material within the dashes may be a word, a phrase, a clause, or a complete sentence. Dashes may also indicate a sudden break or change of thought within a sentence.

> "You told me that he—" I began.

> Our holiday—if you want to call it that—was spent painting the house.

> Captain Smoots—he isn't really a captain—will be your guide.

VII. PARENTHESES

Parentheses, like dashes, set off material which interrupts a sentence. However, they serve to de-emphasize rather than to emphasize the material which they contain.

The speakers at the banquet were Mr. Smithers (Republican) and Mr. Dotson (Democrat).

Phobias are ungrounded fears. (Phobias are discussed more fully in the next chapter.)

VIII. BRACKETS

Brackets set off material inserted by an editor into a direct quotation.

"On the slope to the left there was a long row of guns, *gruff* and *maddened* [italics are mine], denouncing the enemy . . . "

Stephen Crane, *The Red Badge of Courage*
(ed. E. C. Eldridge)

Brackets also contain parenthetic material within parentheses.

The report was sent to William F. Burnell (Republican, California [now at the Los Angeles office]).

IX. APOSTROPHE

Apostrophes are used to form the possessive case of nouns and indefinite pronouns (see p. 29), the plural of figures and words spoken of as words, and contractions.

The collection of the money will be Ruby's responsibility.

You have too many *and*'s in this sentence.

I haven't had a chance to read your book.

Your 7's look like *9*'s.

X. ITALICS

Italics, indicated by continuous underlining in typed or handwritten manuscripts, are used for the titles of all works published under their own names, works of art, foreign words or phrases, names of ships, and words used out of context. (In some instances, words used out of context may be designated by quotation marks instead of by italics.) Italics are also used for emphasis, or to make a word stand out from its context.

Tom Jones is Fielding's best novel.

The *Mona Lisa* was painted by Leonardo.

The *Chryses* won the Bermuda Race.

She couldn't spell the word *vacuum*.

XI.   HYPHEN

1. A hyphen indicates that a word is being divided at the end of a line and being continued on the next line; it is always placed at the end of the line. Consult a dictionary for the correct place to break any word.

2. A hyphen joins two or more words used as a single adjective, and it joins words which are listed as compound words in a dictionary.

   He is a fleet-footed runner.

   The minister delivered a soul-stirring sermon.

   The commander-in-chief of the armed services delivered an address.

   Did you meet Winton's fifteen-year-old daughter?

3. A hyphen separates a prefix ending in a vowel from the basic word beginning with the same vowel (*re-establish, anti-inflationary*). A few words, through usage, have dropped the hyphen (*cooperate, coordinate*).

4. The hyphen combines written two-word numbers from twenty-one to ninety-nine.

XII.   ELLIPSIS

Ellipsis, three spaced dots, is used to indicate the omission of material from a direct quotation. If the last part of a sentence is omitted, the final punctuation is added, and is always included with the ellipsis within the quotation marks.

" . . . *The Old Man and the Sea* was his finest work."

"The play was an overwhelming success. . . ."

"He felt he could not . . . write the book."

XIII. CAPITALIZATION

The practice of capitalization varies a great deal in informal writing, journalistic writing, and formal writing. Following is a list of the most common uses of capitalization in formal writing.

1. Proper nouns: John, New York, Empire State Building, Pacific Ocean.
2. Words derived from proper nouns: American, German, English, Miltonic, Shakespearean.
3. The first word of a sentence or of a line of poetry.
4. The pronoun "I."
5. References to God: Holy Spirit, the Holy One, the Father, He, His.
6. Some abbreviations (see dictionary): M.D., Ph.D., Mr., Jr., Sr.
7. Titles which precede a proper name: President Johnson, Judge Loftus, Lieutenant Ferguson (not: Mr. Smith, President of the club; or Ferguson, a Second Lieutenant.)
8. The first letter of the first and of principal words in titles. Usually articles, short prepositions, and conjunctions are not capitalized in titles.

    Last summer I read Shakespeare's *The Taming of the Shrew,* Miller's *A View from the Bridge,* and Odet's *Waiting for Lefty.*

9. The first word of a complete sentence within quotation marks.

    John asked, "Will you go?"

10. Mother, Father, Uncle, and other indications of family relationships when they are used as proper names.

    May I have a nickel, Mother?

    Uncle Harry visited me last year.

    I always liked Cousin Joe better than my brothers.

11. Sections of the country used as geographical areas.

    The principal cities were in the South.

    I hope to visit the East next summer.

Chapter IV

COMMON ERRORS IN WRITING

The beginning writer may seem to make many errors, but a critical check will usually reveal that he has actually made a few errors but has made them over and over again. By becoming familiar with the relatively few common errors that appear frequently in beginning work and by learning how to avoid them, the student can improve his writing considerably. This book makes no effort to present all the possible errors that a writer might make; rather, it emphasizes the most common grammatical-mechanical errors: errors in grammar, spelling, and punctuation. Only about eight kinds of errors cause the most trouble.

I. FAULTY SUBJECT-VERB RELATIONSHIPS

Students frequently fail to achieve proper subject-verb relationships because they fail to recognize the true subject in the sentence or because they fail to recognize whether the subject is singular or plural.

A. Failure to find the true subject

1. Object of the preposition taken as subject:

   Incorrect: The lady with the children are here.

   Correct: The lady with the children is here.

   Children is the object of the preposition; the subject of the sentence is *lady.* Though she may have the children, they are not necessarily with her. *The lady is here* is what is being stated.

   Incorrect: One of the men are going to get the firewood.

   Correct: One of the men is going to get the firewood.

   Notice that it is not *men* who are going to get the wood, but a man; *one* is going to get the firewood.

2. Expletive *there* taken for subject:

   Incorrect: There are a bouquet of flowers in the vase.

   Correct: There is a bouquet of flowers in the vase.

There is not the subject of the sentence; we are not talking about a "there." Neither is the word *there* an adverb, for it is not really pointing out a location. *There* is a "false subject" because, by its position before the verb, it may mislead a writer; the true subject is *bouquet*.

Incorrect: There is many people in the audience tonight.

Correct: There are many people in the audience tonight.

B. Confusion in number of some special nouns (*Mathematics, politics, economics, physics* are all singular.)

Incorrect: Economics are something that interests me very much.

Correct: Economics is something that interests me very much.

A singular subject should have a singular verb. *Economics* is a singular noun.

Incorrect: For him, mathematics are never easy.

Correct: For him, mathematics is never easy.

General rules for avoiding other but less frequent errors in subject-verb relationships:

1. If the elements of a compound subject are joined by *or* or *nor,* the verb agrees in number with the element closer to it.

   Neither the books nor the pencil is here.

   Either the pencil or the books are here somewhere.

2. Collective nouns name groups and usually take singular verbs. Occasionally, however, the writer may be referring to the individuals or objects within the group. In such cases, the verb is plural.

   The first couple to arrive was ten minutes late.

   The young couple were getting married Saturday afternoon.

II. FRAGMENTS WRITTEN AS SENTENCES

A student will occasionally write a fragment, something less than a sentence, because he mistakes a dependent clause for a sentence or because he fails to provide a subject and a verb. Dependent clauses can usually be identified easily because they begin with a connecting word, which is a signal of subordination.

A. Dependent clause taken as sentence

Incorrect: While his friend was furiously bailing out the boat.

Correct: He watched while his friend was furiously bailing out the boat.

Notice that the introductory word, a subordinate conjunction, makes the statement which follows it dependent.

Incorrect: Because we know that the earth revolves about the sun, and not the other way around.

Correct: Because we know that the earth revolves about the sun, we know the earth to be a satellite.

There is no independent clause in the first sentence.

B. Failure to provide subject or verb or both

Incorrect: The man running quickly down the street to catch the train.

Correct: The man was running quickly down the street to catch the train.

Incorrect: Floating lightly over the peaceful sea in the distance.

Correct: Floating lightly over the peaceful sea in the distance were large fluffy white clouds.

Incorrect: On the other side of the street next to the drug store.

Correct: He stood on the other side of the street next to the drug store.

General rule for avoiding fragments: Be sure that each *sentence* contains a subject and a verb, and be sure that the correct form of the verb is used. Furthermore, be sure that a dependent clause has not been mistaken for a sentence.

III. COMMA FAULTS AND FUSED SENTENCES

The old loose rule of using a comma to indicate a pause in the spoken sentence often causes the student, when writing, to make the serious blunder called the *comma fault:* two sentences separated by only a comma instead of a semicolon or period, or two sentences separated by a comma and a transitional word. A more serious blunder occurs when no punctuation is used between what is actually two sentences. To punctuate correctly clauses employing commas and semicolons, the writer must rely on his understanding of compound and complex sentences.

A. Comma used between independent clauses with no coordinating conjunction (comma fault)

Incorrect: We could not get tickets, they were sold by the time we arrived.

Two independent clauses without a coordinating conjunction joining them should not be joined by a comma.

Incorrect: The woman stood by the open door, she waited for the dog to return.

Correct: The woman stood by the open door; she waited for the dog to return.

B. Comma used between independent clauses with transitional word (*however, moreover, therefore, otherwise, furthermore, nevertheless, hence, thus, yet, still, consequently, meanwhile,* etc.)

Incorrect: The wind is very strong, however, I do not think it will harm anything.

Correct: The wind is very strong; however, I do not think it will harm anything.

Incorrect: They climbed to the top of the peak, meanwhile, their friends made camp in the valley.

Correct: They climbed to the top of the peak; meanwhile, their friends made camp in the valley.

C. No punctuation between two independent clauses (fused sentence)

Incorrect: The rain whipped over the water the wind whistled in the rigging.

Correct: The rain whipped over the water; the wind whistled in the rigging.

Incorrect: He smiled he had finished the project.

Correct: He smiled; he had finished the project.

General rule for avoiding comma faults: Check carefully the internal punctuation of all compound sentences. Use a semicolon if there is no coordinating conjunction between clauses; use a comma if there is a coordinating conjunction.

IV.   LACK OF AGREEMENT IN PRONOUN AND ANTECEDENT

Errors occur in agreement because the student either fails to recognize the true antecedent of a pronoun or does not take into account the number of that antecedent.

A. Failure to recognize true antecedent

Incorrect: She is one of those girls who always does her own work.

Correct: She is <u>one</u> of those girls who always do their own work.

The adjective clause *who always does her own work* does not modify *one;* it modifies *girls.* Hence, it is "girls always do their own work," and the sentence simply says one is among them.

Incorrect: John is the only one of the boys who do the job well.

Correct: John is the <u>only</u> one of the boys who does the job well.

Notice how the use of *the only* changes the sentence. Here the adjective clause *who does the job well* modifies *one,* not *boys.*

B. Number confused with indefinite pronouns

Incorrect: Everybody brought their books to the library on time.

Correct: Everybody brought his books to the library on time.

Although many people are being considered here, each is being considered as an individual: every*body*.

Incorrect: Every person at the picnic wore their sweaters because of the wind.

Correct: Every person at the picnic wore his sweater because of the wind.

General rules for agreement: A personal pronoun must agree with its antecedent in person, number, and gender. (See p. 30.) The indefinite pronouns *anybody, anyone, anything, somebody, someone, something, everybody, everyone, everything, nobody, one, each, either, neither, another* (sometimes *all, some, none*) and the words *person, sort,* and *kind* are singular, and the pronouns referring to these words should be singular.

V. FAULTY REFERENCE OF PRONOUNS

Because the writer knows his own thoughts, he sometimes mistakenly assumes the reader knows them as well. Such an assumption on the part of the writer may cause him to write sentences which contain faulty pronoun reference. He may write a sentence which has the antecedent so far from the pronoun as to cause confusion, he may have only a vague antecedent, or, worse yet, he may have no antecedent at all.

A. Pronoun and antecedent too far apart

Incorrect: The ball rolled down the alley and knocked down the pins, scoring a strike in the first frame; it had hit the first pin a little to the left.

Correct: The ball rolled down the alley and knocked down the pins, scoring a strike in the first frame; the ball had hit the first pin a little to the left.

Incorrect: We saw the sleek sailboat with the tall mast and billowing sails on the far side of the little sheltered harbor; it looked very fast.

Correct: We saw the sleek sailboat with the tall mast and billowing sails on the far side of the little sheltered harbor; the boat looked very fast.

B. Vague antecedent

Incorrect: In the newspaper it says that the Yankees won yesterday.

Correct: The newspaper says the Yankees won yesterday.

The pronoun *it* has an implied, or at best a vague, antecedent. Either some writer or the newspaper is making the pronouncement; the pronoun does not indicate which.

Incorrect: Bill told his friend that he could not find his sister.

Correct: Bill told his friend, "I cannot find your sister."

In the incorrect version the *he* is vague, for it is not clear whether the reference is to Bill or to his friend.

Incorrect: You often find that the one who knows the least says the most.

Correct: One often finds that the one who knows the least says the most.

You can mean only the reader. In the incorrect sentence the statement is that only the reader may find this fact, but the meaning intended is that anyone may find it.

Incorrect: In Alaska you travel about on dogsleds.

Correct: In Alaska people travel about on dogsleds.

C. No antecedent

Incorrect: We went to the aircraft factory to see how they were built.

Correct: We went to the aircraft factory to see how airplanes were built.

The pronoun *they* has no antecedent. We did not go to see how factories are built. The implied antecedent is *airplanes,* and it must be stated.

Incorrect: He put his money in the bank because they pay interest.

Correct: He put his money in the bank because banks pay interest.

General and further rules for avoiding faulty pronoun reference: For clear expression a pronoun must have only one antecedent, and that antecedent must be obvious to the reader.

1. Avoid the indefinite *they, it,* or *you* in formal writing.
2. Avoid reference to an implied antecedent.
3. Avoid using *which, this,* or *that* to refer to the whole idea expressed by some preceding clause or sentence. Usually, in formal writing the antecedent should be a single word.

VI. SHIFTS IN POINT OF VIEW

In an effort to be specific rather than general, a writer sometimes mistakenly shifts the person of a pronoun, or, in an effort to be timely or to give a feeling of urgency, he will incorrectly shift the tense of a verb from past to present tense.

A. Shift in tense of verb

Incorrect: He came jogging down the sidewalk, and he drags the stick over the picket fence.

Correct: He came jogging down the sidewalk, and he dragged the stick over the picket fence.

Incorrect: Then, as we came into the room, we see a man with a bloody hammer in his hand.

Correct: Then, as we came into the room, we saw a man with a bloody hammer in his hand.

B. Shift in person of pronoun

Incorrect: Everyone should take an English class because there you learn how to write.

Correct: Everyone should take an English class because there he learns how to write.

The subject, *everyone,* is in the third person. *You* is in the second person and consequently does not agree. If one avoids the use of "you," such an error is less likely to occur.

Incorrect: The climbers were exhausted; you had to be after going through so many hardships.

Correct: The climbers were exhausted, and well they might be after going through so many hardships.

General rules for correctness in point of view: Be consistent in tenses of verbs. Change tense only when necessary to indicate change in time reference. Do not shift person of pronoun needlessly.

VII. FAULTY MODIFIER

Faulty modifiers usually result from carelessness. In most instances thoughtful reading will reveal them, for they are usually a matter of thoughtlessness rather than of ignorance. .

A. Dangling modifier (does not clearly refer to any word in the sentence)

Incorrect: Reading till 3:00 a.m., the book was finished.

Correct: Reading till 3:00 a.m., we finished the book.

The subject is *book; reading* is a participle which ostensibly modifies it, but a book cannot read. A participle must have a word which it does, in fact, modify, and that word should be close enough to it so as not to cause confusion.

Incorrect: To be a thief, a man's crimes need not be great.

Correct: To be a thief, a man need not commit great crimes.

The subject, *crimes,* cannot be a thief.

B. Misplaced modifier (is not near enough to the word it modifies)

Incorrect: Falling from the branches we saw raindrops.

Correct: We saw raindrops falling from the branches.

In the incorrect version, the participial phrase *falling from the branches,* an adjectival, apparently modifies *we,* for *we* is the nearest nominal to the phrase.

Correctness depends on intent: I *only* said I wanted to go.

I said *only* I wanted to go.

I said I *only* wanted to go.

C. Squinting modifier (creates an ambiguous situation)

Squinting: Bring the papers when ready.

Clear: Bring the papers when you are ready *OR* Bring the papers when they are ready.

Squinting: The airplane pilots were told constantly to be on the alert for flying objects.

Clear: The airplane pilots constantly were told to be on the alert for flying objects *OR* The airplane pilots were told to be constantly on the alert for flying objects.

General rules for avoiding faulty modification: Introductory participles and infinitives should modify clearly some word in the sentence. Check to see that modifiers do not "squint." Adjectives and adverbs, particularly *only, almost, ever, just,* and *even,* should be close to the words they modify.

VIII. MISSPELLING

No other written error incurs the disfavor of a reader so much as an error in spelling, because spelling errors usually indicate carelessness rather than a lack of intelligence. The best remedy for poor spelling is care, concentration, and a desire to improve. When one comes upon a word that he wants to master, he should

1. Look the word up in a dictionary and *memorize its spelling.*
2. Pronounce the word correctly, preferably aloud, while looking at it.
3. Visualize the word, paying particular attention to each letter in sequence.
4. Write the word three times, carefully and correctly.
5. Keep a list of words that have been troublesome and review it frequently.
6. Use newly discovered words whenever it is appropriate to do so. The student should not prefer a familiar word merely because he is sure of its spelling.

General rules for spelling: Because of the great complexity of English, the exceptions to its spelling rules are so numerous as to make many of these rules seem pointless. However, there are four spelling rules which are relatively simple and quite helpful.

1. The ie-ei rule

When the *ie* or *ei* combination has an *ee* sound, the old rhyme sometimes is helpful:

> Write *i* before *e*
> Except after *c.*

When the *ei* combination has a long *a* sound, write *e* before *i.*

relieve	receive	neighbor
niece	conceive	weigh
achieve	deceit	reign

Some exceptions: *either, neither, weird, leisure, seize.*

2. Silent final e

a. Drop the silent final *e* before a suffix beginning with a vowel.

> move — movable
> come — coming
> make — making
> fame — famous

Keep the final *e* in *ce* and *ge* words which retain soft *c* or *g.*

> change — changeable
> notice — noticeable

b. Retain the final *e* to prevent confusion with a similar word or to retain the idea of the basic word.

> dyeing
> singeing
> toeing

c. Retain the final *e* before suffixes beginning with a consonant.

> movement
> hateful
> safely
> nineteen

Some exceptions:

> due — duly
> argue — argument
> true — truly
> awe — awful

3. Final y

a. Words which end in *y* preceded by a consonant change the *y* to *i* before all suffixes except *ing*.

> study   studies   studying
> rely   relied   relying
> apply   applicant   applying
> defy   defiance   defying
> happy   happily

b. Words which end in *y* preceded by a vowel retain the *y* when any suffix is added.

> annoy   annoyed
> monkey   monkeys
> gray   graying
> employ   employable

Some exceptions:

> pay   paid
> day   daily
> say   said
> lay   laid

4. Double the final consonant

All one-syllable words and those multi-syllable words which stress the last syllable, when they end in a single consonant preceded by a

single vowel, double the final consonant when adding a suffix beginning with a vowel.

get	getting
hop	hopping
remit	remitted
control	controller
ram	rammed

Multi-syllable words which do not stress the last syllable do not
double the final consonant.

benefit	benefited
travel	traveled
signal	signaled

Chapter V

WRITING THE ESSAY

It would seem that, armed with adequate information about grammar and with a knowledge of the common writing errors, the writer could face his task with some degree of confidence. Yet we all know that there is a vast difference between knowing grammar, punctuation fundamentals, spelling rules, and common writing errors and being able to organize one's ideas and put them clearly on paper. Good writing is seldom easily done, for it involves the solution of several problems, all of them rather complicated even for experienced writers. These are the problems of content, organization, development, unity, coherence, sentence structure, and, for the beginning writer, the very serious problem of attitude.

THE PROBLEM OF A PROPER ATTITUDE

Achieving and maintaining an attitude conducive to good writing is perhaps the biggest problem for the beginning writer. Frequently, maintaining a proper attitude involves overcoming three improper ones which can be devastating: shyness, boredom, and carelessness. The attitude of shyness comes from the feeling that the writer doesn't have anything of importance to say or that, if he does, he doesn't know how to say it. The first feeling is unfounded, and the second can be corrected.

Even the most inexperienced writer has opinions on a great variety of subjects which, in conversations with his friends, he may have hotly defended. He would never admit to anyone that he never had an opinion worth defending or that he could not defend the opinions he has. His experience has given him a wealth of information. He has witnessed events, heard conversations, read books, newspapers, and magazines, watched television, and listened to teachers; these experiences have left him with many opinions, some of which he holds to tenaciously. Writing is merely the process of putting these views on paper.

If he feels inadequate because he does not know how to express and substantiate these opinions on paper, he needs practice. His feelings of inadequacy the first time he tried to ride a bicycle, drive a car, or play tennis didn't keep him from working at it until he had acquired some degree of proficiency. But he had to work at it. A beginning writer sometimes feels, because he has been using English as long as he can remember, that he should have had practice enough to be able to write well. However, while he has used the language orally a good deal, he has not written much, and writing is the most demanding use of language.

The attitude of boredom is crippling to any writer. It is a particular stumbling block to a student because he must often write when he has no real interest in doing so. As a result, he feels that his only task is to write something that is neat, grammatical, and properly spelled and punctuated. Such a notion allows him to fill his paper with obvious statements and sweeping generalities unworthy of him and of the task confronting him; it makes his paper vague and incoherent rather than clear and logical. A good writer must somehow become involved in what he is doing.

The attitude of carelessness makes a shambles of what might otherwise have been a worthwhile paper. It is amazing that people who take great care to impress others by good grooming, meticulous housekeeping, or circumspect behavior should take such little thought of exposing disorderly minds by careless writing. The careless writer may imagine that his audience will be sympathetic, but no such sympathy exists. A good writer is one who treats his reader as a guest; he must do everything he can to set his house in order.

THE PROBLEM OF CONTENT

The general content of a paper is usually determined by circumstances rather than by whim. The student must write a laboratory report, a letter, a research paper in a given area, an examination, or an essay on some subject determined by a teacher. He must also produce several kinds of writing: descriptions, narrations, autobiographical sketches, reports, arguments, or explanations. More often than not, in formal situations he will write an explanation or an argument. Because the description, the narration, and the autobiographical sketch present a different kind of problem, in this chapter we will deal only with argument and explanation, and we will deal with argument only to the extent of showing how to organize facts and ideas to support a particular point of view.

The work of a beginning writer is frequently bad because he either writes about something obvious or trivial or merely lists a series of facts without using them for a purpose. A student required to write a paper about television might include much information about programs, commercials, and audiences, yet he might leave the reader wondering what the writer is driving at. It might be necessary in some cases to write a paper in which a listing of facts is all that is required, a report of some kind, but most of our writing demands more. It demands that a writer do something with facts: organize them, use them to support some point of view. The point of view is the essence of what the writer has to say. The student who is writing about television, for example, could say "Television commercials are ruining television," or "Television programs give youngsters a wealth of information," or "Television is detrimental to the health and welfare of children." It is this point of view that gives the paper purpose and direction, and it is the support of the point of view which gives the paper validity and vitality.

The Thesis. Determining a point of view toward a subject is the most important step a writer has to take in writing, for to a large extent it determines the success of his work. This point of view should be stated in one sentence, the *thesis*. Consequently, the writer must give much thought to which of many possible theses he will develop.

Which thesis to choose is determined by the writer's interest, his knowledge or what source materials are available, and the amount of time and space at his disposal. He would be foolish to take a thesis in which he has no interest, even though it may seem at the time an easy idea to support, because if he does so he is almost sure to write a bad paper. Furthermore, he would be foolish to take a thesis which he could not support by his own experience or by research. His whole purpose in writing is to convince a reader of the validity of his thesis, and this takes adequate and specific information. He would also be foolish to take a thesis which was so broad that he had neither time nor space to support it. And certainly he would be foolish to take a thesis the truth of which was so obvious that once he stated his position he could do nothing more than write variations of the same sentence.

Many writers, in attempting to write forceful, brief theses, oversimplify, leaving themselves with a proposition that is rather difficult to support. If the writer chooses the thesis "The caliber of our television programs is determined by what sells toothpaste," he will be ignoring some rather splendid programs that don't sell toothpaste at all. It would admittedly be much easier to ignore these programs, but ignoring them will certainly weaken his argument. Obviously he must qualify his thesis in some way: "Most television programs are bad because they are leveled at mass audiences." Although the thesis must be stated simply and precisely, it must be completely defensible.

Limiting the Topic. Once the writer has accepted a thesis, he has limited the topic. If he accepts the thesis stated in the previous paragraph, he should not write about how much a television set saves on the monthly entertainment bill, or whether or not a color television set is worth the extra money it costs, or whether or not television repairmen can be trusted, regardless of how much these matters may interest him.

Organizing Support for the Thesis. Having the thesis in mind, preferably written on a piece of scratch paper, the writer is ready to gather and arrange his support. He would be wise to jot down on scratch paper the two or three (or more, depending on the length of the paper) reasons why he believes that his thesis is true. These reasons should be his answer to the inevitable question a listener might ask: "What makes you think that your statement is true?" If any of his stated reasons do not answer that question, they should be omitted. What the writer ends up with might look like this:

> *Thesis:* Most television programs are bad because they are leveled at mass audiences.
>
> I. Television programs are supported by sponsors who use them as a medium of advertising.
>
> II. To be successful, advertising must reach the largest possible audience.
>
> III. To reach the largest possible audience, programs must cater to the tastes of the majority.

If the writer can prove I, II, and III by his own experience or by his reading, he has in fact proved the thesis, and that is precisely what he set out to do.

THE PROBLEM OF ADEQUATE DEVELOPMENT

When the outline has been sketched out, the writer is ready to develop his paper. Every paper has three essential parts: a beginning, a middle, and an ending. The outline, when it is fully developed, forms the middle or the body of the paper. To it must be added an introduction and a conclusion.

The Beginning. A writer is obliged to meet the reader wherever the reader is. Usually the writer has a specific reader in mind: his employer, his teacher, a friend, a colleague. If he hasn't, he must imagine the person his reader is likely to be. He must then take care to involve that reader in the subject and to make clear to him the purpose of the paper. Such is the function of the introduction.

How does one get any reader involved in the subject of a paper? One way is to begin with such a sensational burst that whatever follows is bound to be anticlimactic, but of course that method is not effective. A better method is to indicate how the subject already involves the reader or how it can interest him. At any rate, the reader must be convinced by the introduction that reading the remainder of the paper will be worth the trouble it takes.

An introduction must lead very clearly and logically to the thesis. By leading up to the thesis, it will give the reader an idea of where the paper is going, a notion of what to expect. The task suggests that the introduction begin with some rather general statements of interest to the reader, narrowing gradually to a statement of the thesis. In a diagram it would look like this.

X   Thesis

Finally, the introduction should contain any definitions needed to make the thesis precise or any qualifications needed to make it true. In our example, the qualification that some television programs are good has been implied in the thesis. Further expansion of this idea is certainly demanded in the introduction.

Poor introductions have two common weaknesses: poor development and overdevelopment.

Poor Development. An introduction must be relatively well developed if it is to be effective. It must be something more than a bald statement of the thesis. We can easily see that two or three sentences cannot involve the reader in the subject and then lead him smoothly to the thesis.

Overdevelopment. An introduction can be overdeveloped in two ways. It can include within it the support of the thesis, support which logically belongs in the body of the paper, or it can overshadow by sheer length the remainder of the paper, leaving a head much too large for the body.

The Middle. The middle of the paper consists of the supporting points of the outline, fully developed. Just as the thesis needs logical support, so each of the supporting points in the outline needs logical support. A writer cannot ask the reader to accept the thesis or its supporting sentences at face value. The strength of his paper lies in how well he uses facts to back up these generalizations, and it is precisely here that many papers collapse. Too many beginning writers are content to flesh out paragraphs with nothing more than a few generalizations, each of which in turn needs to be supported.

It is in the developing paragraph that the writer must draw on his own experience and reading to justify his thesis. Unfortunately he finds it much easier to write a little about a lot than to write a lot about a little. Good writing has an intensity about it, an intellectual toughness brought about by including much information in a small space. If the writer deals only in generalities, he dissipates the intensity of his work, and his work no longer has the power to convince the reader that the writer knows what he is talking about. His paper will be only a fleshless outline.

Each supporting point may be developed in only one paragraph or in several paragraphs, depending upon the length of the paper. Actually, each supporting point becomes the thesis for an essay within an essay, for that is precisely what a paragraph is. The thesis of the paragraph is stated in its topic sentence, and the paragraph as a whole needs the same kind of careful organization that the entire paper demands. It must begin interestingly, the middle must support the topic sentence, and it must end naturally. Although the topic sentence may appear anywhere within the paragraph, in ninety per cent of all paragraphs the topic sentence is the first sentence.

In our sample outline, the first sentence after the introduction would be "Television programs are supported by the successful advertising of their sponsors." It would then be up to the writer to prove by his own experience or reading that this statement is true. He would have to indicate the size or extent of the advertiser's investment and the stake which the advertiser has in the program he is sponsoring. The reader must be convinced that the sponsors of television programs are in the business of selling products and not in the business of improving the aesthetic values of the viewing public.

So it is with every paragraph. The support of the topic sentence rests upon fact, and a fact is a statement which needs no further proof. If the writer knows some facts which seem to negate the topic sentence, he cannot ignore them; he must somehow qualify his topic sentence to include them, or he must refute them. If he ignores them, the reader can claim that the writer holds to the topic sentence and to the thesis only out of ignorance.

If the paragraph is to have a tight structure, every sentence in it must carry its share of the support for the topic sentence. Such a paragraph has unity. To digress is always tempting, especially when the writer thinks of some delightful sentence which just cries to be written. Such digressions, however, divert the reader's attention from the business at hand, thereby defeating the intention of the writer.

Paragraphs may vary in length from one sentence to more than 350 words. One thing is certain, however. A short paragraph, unless used for transition or emphasis, is usually not convincing. If the writer finds a short paragraph on his hands, he can do one of three things: he can seek further information to support the topic sentence, he can combine the paragraph with another paragraph of similar content, or he can omit the paragraph altogether. If it cannot be expanded or combined, it is probably not significant enough to be included.

The Ending. The conclusion is a relatively short but important part of every paper. In very short papers, the conclusion may be merely the last sentence of the last paragraph; in longer papers, it may be from one to several paragraphs. Regardless of its length, the conclusion is the device which brings the paper to a satisfactory ending.

In longer papers, the conclusion may be almost an inversion of the introduction, with the thesis being the first sentence instead of the last. The rest of the conclusion may be a recapitulation of the most important points of the paper, or it may be an expansion of the thesis. In any case, it ties together any loose ends and makes sure that the reader cannot miss the point which the paper makes.

Three errors are found frequently in poor conclusions. One is the introduction of a new idea which is irrelevant to the thesis. Another is the ostensible summary which is not a summary at all but a distortion of what was presented in the body of the paper. Another is a needless repetition of points which are already firmly fixed in the reader's mind. The good conclusion, rather than belaboring the obvious, leaves the reader with something worthwhile to think about.

THE PROBLEM OF UNITY

What we have been discussing all along really has to do with the problem of unity. A unified paper is one which sticks to supporting a thesis; a unified paragraph is one which sticks to supporting a topic sentence. If the topic sentences truly support the thesis, and if all the sentences in each paragraph truly support the topic sentence, the paper has unity. A unified paper helps the reader to keep the thesis in mind throughout the entire paper.

THE PROBLEM OF COHERENCE

Coherence depends first upon a logical sequence of ideas. At times the relationship of these ideas must be indicated by some means besides sequence alone.

The first requisite of coherence within a paragraph is unity, but a paragraph may have unity and still not have coherence. A writer must take the trouble to see that his sentences flow smoothly from one to another. The sentences first must be placed in order, organized in a logical time or space sequence or in a logical development of ideas. The paragraph must start interestingly and end naturally. Mechanical devices are helpful in making paragraphs coherent, but these devices cannot connect sentences which by their content are incompatible. The following mechanical devices are useful:

1. Repetition of key words
2. Repetition of an idea
3. Use of a pronoun whose antecedent appears in a preceding sentence
4. Parallel sentence structure
5. Transitional words and phrases (see pp. 42, 47)

As sentences within paragraphs must be ordered to achieve smoothness and emphasis, so must paragraphs within the total essay. Such transitional signals as "in the first place," "another consideration," and "finally" are helpful, but again, they are helpful only if the paragraph arrangement is logical. The place to arrange the paragraphs in their proper order is in the outline, for there the writer can see which ideas are most important, which idea would make a good beginning, and which one would make a good ending. It is wise to close with an important idea so that the paper can build toward a climax.

THE PROBLEM OF POINT OF VIEW

In addition to being unified and coherent, a paper must maintain a consistent point of view. Every writer is addressing an audience from some point in time and for some particular purpose. He must adapt his language both to the audience and to his purpose for writing. He would not use the language of a research paper in a letter to a close personal friend, nor can he use informal English in his research paper. In both cases his language would be inappropriate, and inappropriate English at its worst obscures meaning, at its best diverts a reader's interest from the writer's ideas.

In addition, a writer is addressing his subject from some point in time and space. He cannot indiscriminately change the tense of verbs or the person and number of pronouns. If he writes carelessly, he may write such sentences as "The average television viewer has demanded a program that they understood with little effort," rather than "The average television viewer has demanded a program that he can understand with little effort." Careless use of verbs and pronouns creates confusion, and that is the last thing a writer wants to create.

THE PROBLEM OF WRITING GOOD SENTENCES

Good papers rest ultimately upon good sentences, sentences which are alive, interesting, and provocative. English is a rich language that gives us a variety of ways to express ourselves. It is a shame that we so easily fall into ruts, using worn-out words in dull sentences. Instead of using our imaginations to stimulate those with whom we are communicating, we use the words that come first into our minds. All too frequently our sentences become a perpetual word-association test, each word suggesting the one to follow, instead of planned structures calculated to hold the reader's attention.

Although we cannot write good sentences merely by following a formula, we can learn a few basic devices which will make our sentences more interesting and forceful. Good sentences usually include words which are concrete rather than abstract, specific rather than general. It is much easier to write "They advertise a lot of things on television" than "Sponsors on television advertise everything from beer to bras, funeral plots to Western ranches." The whole purpose of writing is to convey an idea from writer to reader as vividly and precisely as possible. In order to do so, the writer must use the whole range of language, not simply the words which are easiest to recall. The more sense images he can create through concrete, specific words, the more he will involve the reader by appealing to his experiences.

The following examples illustrate the preciseness of specific concrete words.

General: a *nice* party

Specific: *interesting, wild, exciting, orderly, exotic*

General: *walked* slowly

Specific: *shuffled, sauntered, dawdled, meandered*

Abstract: *dwelling*

Concrete: *hotel, apartment, home, mansion, igloo, shack*

A word of caution: many writers feel that their writing is enhanced if sentences are complicated and contain big words. As a result of such thinking, they seek complexity for its own sake, writing things they would never say, a jumble of words which defy the reader to extricate from them any clear idea. Good writers are usually direct. Every word has to carry its weight; none is used merely for effect. A good test for any sentence is "Would I say this sentence to the person I am writing to?"

WRITING VARIED SENTENCES

As we have seen in Chapter II, most sentences in the English language fall into one of four basic sentence patterns. If we violate these patterns indiscriminately, our writing becomes confusing and awkward. On the other hand, if our only concern is to write simple, grammatical sentences, we might very well end up with the primer style: "The girl has a dog. The girl is Jane. The dog is Rover. See Jane. See Rover." Between the extremes of awkward sentence variation and the primer style we have a wide choice of devices which can make our sentences more emphatic and interesting. Among them are the use of subordination, phrases, appositives, absolute constructions, interruptors, parallel structure, and variation in length.

Subordination

The real problem of the primer style of writing, aside from sheer boredom, is that all ideas appear to be of equal importance.

Bill ran down the street. His dog ran after him. There was a lot of traffic.

Through subordination the writer can indicate which idea he wants to emphasize.

Bill ran down the street through the heavy traffic, his dog running after him.

When Bill ran down the street through the heavy traffic, his dog ran after him.

Although the traffic was heavy, Bill ran down the street, his dog running after him.

Appositives (see p. 27)

Appositives add detail.

Last night we met Bill's neighbor, a retired Navy officer who looked at life through a porthole.

Participial Phrases (see pp. 33, 35)

Participial phrases provide variety in structure and are a means of subordinating.

Wiping the lipstick from his upper lip and backing away from his secretary's desk, Bill sheepishly said hello to his wife.

The dean, looking more like a funeral director than a college administrator, extended his hand to the new student.

Absolute Constructions (see p. 43)

Absolute constructions provide another means of subordination.

The old man watched his daughter leave, his hand making a hopeless circle in the air.

Weather permitting, all of us will take a fifty-mile hike.

The car stopped, its radiator belching steam, its tail pipe smoking.

Interruptors

Normal sentence patterns can be varied by words or phrases which interrupt the normal cadence.

He will, of course, accept the invitation.

We left at three o'clock in the morning—why I'll never know—and arrived in time to wait two hours for a ranger.

Parallel Structure

Parallel structure is the deliberate repetition of similar grammatical structures in series. It is one of the most effective ways of making sentences interesting, emphatic, and varied. We use it daily in our conversation; good writing is filled with splendid examples.

I have taken courses in physics, chemistry, biology, and zoology.

My favorite authors are Faulkner, Salinger, and Camus.

He walked into the library, picked up a book, and began leafing through the pages.

The Lord is my shepherd. I shall not want;
He maketh me to lie down in green pastures,

He leadeth me beside the still waters,

He restoreth my soul.

The best and clearest thinking in the world is done and the finest art is produced, not by men who are hungry, ragged and harrassed, but by men who are well-fed, warm and easy in mind.

H. L. Mencken

Varying Length

The use of too many sentences of approximately the same length will result in monotony. Variation from long to short will add greatly to the interest of a series of sentences. Short sentences are particularly useful as means of emphasis at strategic points throughout a paper because they act as punctuation marks. Like this. Because it keeps the reader interested in what is going on, sentence variety serves the overall purpose of the paper.

THE PROBLEM OF REVISING

Many people feel that when they place a period after the last sentence of their papers their task is completed. What they have written somehow calcifies and defies change. Or they feel that they have already done the best that they can do; there is no sense in going over their work. Needless to say, such notions are foolish. Every writer, no matter how experienced, should take time to revise his work. The more conscientious he is, the more he will feel that he can yet make his work better.

However, it is rather fruitless to go over the work if the writer does not look for some specific errors he is likely to have made. Each of us is prone to make certain types of errors, and we should take care to find out what our weaknesses are. The checklist inside the back cover will help the student avoid some specific writing errors, and, of course, the previous chapter points out the most common grammatical errors.

Here are two short essays on the same general topic. One is a relatively bad essay, the other a relatively good one. Comments follow each essay.

The Advantages of Television

There are many advantages to television. Some of them are better than others.

First of all, television brings many sports events to the fans. The World Series is on in the fall, and it is always good. Last year the Dodgers beat the mighty Yankees four straight. Baseball is all right, but I personally prefer football. I won three letters in football in high school, even though my team never won a championship.

British television is quite different from American television, because it is controlled by the government. It has three different kinds of programs, each aimed at a different audience. The first is rather high-brow, the second middle-brow, and the third low-brow. It features such performers as the Beatles. I think they are terrible singers and thoroughly nauseous. What is even worse is the way the young girls scream when the Beatles play and sing.

They did the same sort of thing when Elvis Presley used to sing. Disgusting.

Television is a good trade these days. Almost everyone has a set, and they are always getting out of whack. Usually television repairmen get good wages. This is one of the greatest advantages of television. John Carol, a friend of mine, took some courses in electronics and found a job right away. He married a girl he met while he was repairing a set. So you can see that this is a great advantage of television.

The worst thing is the commercials. They tell you that the products will get you a girl, but I notice I haven't. All that business about roll-on deodorants is mostly nonsense. The best kind of deodorant is the spray, because it gets through the hair right to the skin. No one likes a person who smells badly. Beer commercials are misleading, since most of the beer ads show more bubbles than beer actually has.

I like television, but I don't watch it too much. I think a person should get some exercise instead of just sitting there looking at a western. I prefer handball, though I usually play more golf.

Comment. Although this paper contains no misspelled words, no grammatical errors, and no errors in mechanics, it is obviously an unsatisfactory paper because the writer is unable to stick to his point. He may have had a general idea of how to develop his thesis about the advantages of television, but he soon loses the thread of his argument. Commercials, for instance, can hardly be considered an advantage of television.

Furthermore, the paragraphs are not unified or coherent. Each begins with a sentence which might be a key sentence, but the following sentences wander off into largely irrelevant bypaths. Although the writer sometimes does, as in paragraph five, try to get back to his point, he is never very successful in doing so. Sometimes he includes two ideas, as in paragraph six, without proper indication that they are related (deodorants and beer).

In addition, the paragraphs display a distressing lack of the kind of coherence that can be achieved by means of careful pronoun reference. For instance, the second sentence of the fifth paragraph has "they," for which there is no antecedent. Errors of this kind can lead only to confusion.

All in all the paper is a failure because of bad rhetorical practices. Correctness in mechanical detail is not enough; good writing demands organization and control over idea as well.

The Advantages of Television

Television, like death and taxes, is apparently here to stay. While admittedly a time-consuming and largely worthless pursuit much of the time, it does have certain strong points in its favor, and a discriminating viewer can find much to admire.

In the first place, TV does help us to stay abreast of the world of which we are a part. Like a daily newspaper but in some respects better, it can make us aware of the racial tensions in Birmingham, the sex scandals in Britain, and the brush-fire wars in South Viet Nam and elsewhere. On certain occasions, such as the orbiting of the astronauts, it can engage the whole world for long periods of time, giving men and women everywhere a sense of participation in the exciting and important events of our time. Without TV we would be less aware of what goes on around us, and worse for our lack.

Television is sometimes a medium for serious art, too, a special kind of drama with a kinship to both the stage and the cinema but different from either. Although most programs on television are not very artistic or very serious in their attempt to present significant human experiences, enough are so that some judicious choosing can result in a diet high in excellent TV fare. The Playhouse 90 series, now unhappily terminated, is an example of what TV can do at its best. The U. S. Steel Hour was another fine series. Specials of various kinds, like Ingrid Bergman in *Hedda Gabler,* are scheduled from time to time, and frequently they abundantly repay the time taken to scan the weekly TV guide to spot and plan ahead for the worthwhile programs. Anyone interested in serious television art will really have little trouble finding it.

Even when it isn't particularly rewarding as art, TV is often amusing or entertaining enough to justify a few hours in front of a set. The World Series on TV, for instance, gives millions a chance to take part in our national idiocy rather than just the few who can get into the ball park. Programs like The Dobie Gillis Show and The Dick Van Dyke Show, while they probably have no lasting value as art, do provide a laugh or two—not a bad idea in our world of tensions. And who can resist once in a while watching those intrepid pioneers winning the West on Wagon Train? Or Brett and Bart winning the pot on Maverick? It is true that TV devotes most of its time to mere entertainment, but sometimes the entertainment is worthy of our attention.

So let us not be too hard on the vast wasteland that is TV most of the time. Let us recognize that a significant part of the time TV is worth watching. If we watch it when it isn't, should the blame fall on TV or elsewhere?

Comment. The opening sentence is used to gain interest and to establish the subject—television. The second sentence serves as a thesis statement for the composition. Notice the qualifications and limitations of the topic by such key words as "worthless," "time-consuming," "much," "does have," "points," and "favor." We can see clearly that the writer is going to present "points" in favor of TV, although both reader and writer are aware—"admittedly"—that there is much worthless material broadcast.

The phrase "in the first place" acts as a transition to get us into the first point. The first sentence of the second paragraph serves as a topic sentence. It is the assertion that TV keeps us informed. This topic sentence is developed by the next two sentences by a simple comparison and several examples, and the last sentence in the paragraph concludes the first point.

In the third paragraph, once more the opening sentence serves as the topic sentence by introducing the new point, art. Notice how the word "too" serves as a transition for carrying over to a new idea and at the same time adding conviction to the positive assertion of the thesis—"strong points in . . . favor." Once again the topic sentence is developed, but now with a qualification: "most programs on television are not very artistic." A series of specific examples follows, though, which does substantiate the view that TV is sometimes a medium for serious art. Once again the final sentence concludes the paragraph.

The clause opening the fourth paragraph serves as a transition, and the remainder of the sentence establishes the topic. The next four sentences give examples "to justify a few hours in front of a set," and the final sentence effectively concludes the paragraph.

The brief final paragraph serves as a conclusion to the whole composition. The reader knows that no more points are to follow, and he is left with the thought that a thing need not be bad, but the abuse of a thing may make it bad.

Generally speaking, the organization of the composition is good. The paper has a beginning, a middle, and an end. It has unity—it sticks to the thesis. It has coherence—it is clear and logical, flowing from one point to the next. It has emphasis—it moves from the important informative value of TV through quality entertainment to casual amusement.

The style of the paper is appropriate to the attitude; the style is that of the informal essay. It is neither pretentious nor vulgar; it is altogether appropriate for the topic, for the writer, and for the probable audience.

GLOSSARY OF USAGE

Unabridged dictionaries, like the recently published third edition of *Webster's New International Dictionary,* attempt to record all of the standard current words in the English language. Every word spoken or written by an English-speaking person using his own language has a legitimate place in a dictionary, no matter what the word's origin, its acceptance among various segments of society, or its frequency of occurrence. As long as it is a living part of a living language, every word should be recorded.

The record—not what a word *should* mean or how it *should* be used, but what it *does* mean and how it *is* used—is a rather large one, so large, in fact, that an unabridged dictionary, as important as it is as a record, is not the most useful aid to a writer who wants to find some kinds of information, particularly if he is in a hurry. Various abridgements of unabridged dictionaries are one solution to the problem. At least they are portable, and they contain entries which the abridgers think will be of most use to the people the different abridgements are prepared for: high school students, college students, secretaries, and the like.

Even these abridgements, however, have their limitations. Sometimes they include too much material, and one has to waste time digging out what he needs. Sometimes they do not include the material wanted, and one wastes time in fruitless search. Because of their strictly alphabetical arrangement, they often do not point out some of the most informative relationships between words or distinguish between words likely to be confused. Consequently, a selective list of words briefly defined and conveniently arranged can often save a writer much time. Such a list of words, augmented with a few phrases, is presented here.

In using this glossary, the writer should keep some important facts in mind:

1. It is prepared for the writer, and assumes a need for a relatively formal rather than an informal or colloquial language. What we say and what we write in more or less formal situations demand different vocabularies and different degrees of precision; the entries here guide the user to precise, relatively formal written English, like that found in books, serious journals, and the editorial pages of a good newspaper.

2. The entries are rather prescriptive in their phrasing. "Avoid this" or "Do not say that" obviously must mean "On most occasions, unless there is

a very good reason for using it instead of the more conventional or more widely acceptable form, avoid this" or "Except in unusual circumstances, most discriminating, educated people do not use that construction in formal writing, so probably you should not do so." The prescriptive tone arises not from a mistaken idea that language levels are inviolable or that certain words are intrinsically better than others but from the necessity for brevity. Most people in looking up a word in a glossary do not want a dissertation on it, or even a choice of several possibilities; they want an answer, the shorter the better. This the list provides, with only as much information as is necessary.

3. None of the entries here is complete. Many of the entries try only to make distinctions between words frequently confused. Complete information must be sought in standard dictionaries or in one of the more comprehensive usage guides listed in the bibliography.

4. The entries were chosen on the basis of experience: all deal with frequently made errors or answer frequently asked questions. No doubt some of the entries will be more useful than others, but all represent common usage problems.

No absolutely "right" usage exists. The items included here probably reflect the training, experience, and bias of the editors, who have been deliberately conservative in making their choices. They feel that most people ought to avoid innovations in language usage. The average writer can operate comfortably within the choices here, and can save his major mental energy for more important things, like thinking about what he wants to convey.

5. All entries with multiple items are cross indexed except those in which the multiple items would be consecutive entries anyway, e. g. *bridal, bridle.*

6. The items which most often give trouble are starred in the primary entry. For instance, the confusion between *to* and *too, its* and *it's, their* and *there* continues despite all attempts of English teachers to explain the important distinctions between them; such items are starred.

7. The pronunciation symbols are self-explanatory.

8. The part of speech of an entry, if not stated, is implicit in the explanation or example.

a, an, the   The articles or noun indicators. When used, they always precede a noun or the modifiers before a noun: *an elephant, the huge stone, a very large, dark woman.*

    A and *an* are the indefinite articles, referring not to one item in particular but to any one item in a general class: *Fido is a dog. Here is an egg. A* and *an* are both singular. *A* is used before words which begin with a consonant sound: *a dog. An* is used before words which begin with a vowel sound: *an egg.* Some letters, particularly *u,* which usually indicate vowel sounds, actually act as consonants in some words: *a European trip, a useful tool.* Go by the sound, not the spelling. Use *a* before words which begin with a sounded *h: a history book.* Use *an* when the *h* is not sounded: *an honest man.*

The is the definite article, referring to one specific item: *Fido is the dog that bit me. The egg spoiled in the nest. The* is either singular or plural.

absolutely   Avoid as an intensifier meaning *exceedingly.*

accelerate, exhilarate   To *accelerate* is to increase speed; to *exhilarate* is to increase excitement.

*accept, except   To *accept* is to receive; to *except* is to exclude. *Accept* is a verb; *except* is a verb and a preposition: *I shall except no one from my lists. All except John went to town.*

access, excess   An *access* is a means to entry; *excess* is more than enough, lack of moderation.

A. D., B. C.   *Anno Domini* (in the year of the Lord) and *before Christ.* Use only with dates: *44 B. C., A. D. 55,* not *four hundred years A.D.* Usually A. D. may be dispensed with: *688* means *A. D. 688* unless otherwise indicated. Recent dates rarely use A. D.

ad, add   *Ad* is short for *advertisement;* don't use it in formal writing. To *add* is to increase in number.

adapt, adept, adopt   To *adapt* is to make adjustments, as to situations. One who is *adept* is either skilled or proficient. To *adopt* is to make something one's own: *James was adept enough to adapt to the situation when Mary wanted to adopt a child.*

add   See *ad.*

adept, adopt   See *adapt.*

adverse, averse   *Adverse* is opposite or contrary; *averse* is unwilling. *Averse* is usually used with *to: I am averse to that course of action.*

advice, advise   To *advise* is to give counsel; the *advice* is the counsel given.

*affect, effect   To *affect* is to change. An *effect* is a result. To *effect* is to bring about something: *His action cannot affect us. What effect will his actions have? I hope they will effect a change.*

afterward, afterwards   These are interchangeable forms of the same adverb.

aggravate To *aggravate* is to make worse. It should not be used to mean to annoy or to irritate: not *He aggravates me,* but *He aggravated an already tense situation* or *He aggravated the wound.*

aisle, isle An *aisle* is a space left for walking between seats. An *isle* is an island.

alibi Technically, *alibi* is a legal term indicating that the accused was not at the scene of the crime when the crime he is charged with was committed. Do not use the word imprecisely to mean any excuse.

all . . . not, not . . . all *All men are not honest* is not the same as *Not all men are honest.* Use *not* with precision.

allusion, illusion An *allusion* is an indirect reference. An *illusion* is a false image, a misconception.

*all right The only acceptable spelling.

alley, ally An *alley* is an access road usually at the back of the lots in a city block. An *ally* is a confederate, usually in a military alliance.

allowed, aloud To be *allowed* is to be permitted. *Aloud* means audible: *He stopped whispering and spoke aloud.*

ally See *alley.*

all ready, already If all are prepared, they are *all ready. Already* means having happened previously or prior to a particular time: *Are the girls all ready already?*

all together, altogether If all are together, they are *all together. Altogether* means completely: *When we were all together, we were altogether in agreement.*

all ways, always *All ways* means in every possible way. *Always* means perpetually, all the time: *We always tried all ways to win the games.*

*almost, most *Almost* means nearly. *Most* means almost all. *Most* should not be used for *almost.*

a lot, lots In the meaning of *much* or *many,* not appropriate for the most formal levels of writing but acceptable elsewhere. *A lot* is two words, not to be confused with the verb *allot,* to apportion.

aloud See *allowed.*

already See *all ready.*

altar, alter An *altar* is a structure used in worship. To *alter* means to change.

although, though As subordinating conjunctions the words are interchangeable: *Though (or although) I am tired, I will go to the store for you. .Although* is the more frequently used in this way. *Though* also functions as a transition word or sentence modifier: *I caught four* *fish. Two were too small to keep, though.* In this use, *though* usually comes at the end of the clause.

altogether See *all together*.

always See *all ways*.

A. M., P. M., a. m., p. m. May be either capitals or lower case. The initials represent *ante meridiem* (before noon) and *post meridiem* (after noon). Use only with numbers: *3 p. m., 7:10 A. M., five p. m.* Do not say *six in the p. m.* Do not use with *o'clock:* not *5 o'clock p. m.,* but *5 p. m.*

among, amongst Interchangeable forms of the same word.

among, between Use *among* when dealing with more than two items, *between* when dealing with two: *Between the two nations there was good will. There was considerable strife among the factions of the party.* This distinction is often neglected except in the most formal writing. *Amongst* is also correct.

*amount, number Use *amount* and words implying amount for material that comes in bulk and cannot be counted: *a large amount of sugar.* Use *number* and words implying number for items that can be counted: *a large number of crystals.* Similarly, *less sugar* and *fewer crystals.* But *more sugar* and *more crystals.*

ampersand Do not use the ampersand (&) to replace *and* in any written text. It may be used in charts and tables.

an, and Do not confuse these words even though in rapid speech they may sound alike. See *a*.

and, as well as, together with *And* is a coordinating conjunction. It may not be replaced by *as well as* or *together with* in creating plurals: *The boy and his sister come here often. The boy together with his sister comes here often. The boy as well as his sister comes here often.*

and etc. Since *et cetera* means *and so forth,* the *and* in *and etc.* is superfluous and incorrect.

angel, angle *Angels* are in heaven. *Angles* are the meetings of lines.

ante-, anti- These prefixes mean respectively *before* and *against: ante-bellum* and *anti-war*.

anxious, eager To be *anxious* is to look forward with dread or apprehension. To be *eager* is to look forward with hope or delight: *When you didn't come home for supper, I was very anxious to hear what was wrong. I was eager for my birthday to come.*

anyway, anyways The first form is correct, the second incorrect.

anywhere, anywheres The first form is correct, the second incorrect.

appraise, apprise   To *appraise* is to set a value upon. To *apprise* is to inform; it is usually used with *of: He was apprised of the danger.*

apt, likely   *Apt* means fitting or suitable. *Likely* means probable: *That was an apt answer. He is likely to go to pieces under pressure.*

are, our   Do not confuse these really very dissimilar words just because they are often carelessly pronounced alike.

aren't I?   *Aren't I* is an uneasy replacement for the somewhat awkward and stiff but correct *Am I not? Ain't I?* is not yet considered standard despite its filling an obvious need in the language.

arise, rise   To *arise* is to get up, or, in a metaphorical sense, to come into being: *A quarrel may arise over nothing.* To *rise* can mean to arise or to move upward: *Hot air will naturally rise.*

around, round   *Round* is used as an adjective to mean either circular or spherical. It may also in some circumstances mean *around. Around* is used as a preposition meaning on all sides: *I walked around the block.* It can also mean *approximately: We left around eight o'clock. Around* can also be an adverb: *I'll be around.*

as   Avoid as a subordinating conjunction meaning *because:* not *I had to do it, as I was the oldest* but *I had to do it because I was the oldest.*

ascent, assent   An *ascent* is a climb, an *assent* an act of agreeing.

as good or better than   This and other such constructions which combine the positive and comparative degrees of modifiers are illogical and awkward, and should be avoided: not *He is as good or better than I am* but *He is as good as or better than I am* or *He is as good as I am, or better.*

as well as   See *and.*

at   The *at* is undesirable in such constructions as *Where is he at?* Delete it.

aural, oral   *Aural* pertains to the sense of hearing; *oral* means spoken. We detect oral communication by aural means.

averse   See *adverse.*

avocation, vocation   An *avocation* is what one does for fun when he is not working at his work, his *vocation.*

a while, awhile   Both mean for a short time and may be used interchangeably.

back of, in back of   *Behind* means the same and is more economical.

backward, backwards   As adverbs, the two are interchangeable. *Backward* is the adjective form: *He comes from a backward country.*

***bad, badly**   *Bad* is the adjective form and should be used in the predicate position after linking verbs: *I feel bad. She looks bad. Badly* is an adverb: *I slept badly. I feel badly* is often heard but should be avoided in formal writing.

bail, bale　*Bail* is security for a released prisoner. A *bale* is a bundle, as of cotton. To *bail* is to ladle out, as water from a boat.

bare, bear　*Bare* means naked, without covering. To *bear* means to carry. A *bear* is an animal.

barely　See *can barely.*

bazaar, bizarre　A *bazaar* is a market place in the Near East, or a special event, usually in churches, for selling miscellaneous goods. *Bizarre* means strange or outlandish.

B. C.　See *A. D.*

beach, beech　A *beach* is sand at the seashore; a *beech* is a kind of tree.

bear　See *bare.*

beat, beet　To *beat* is to pummel or whip. A *beet* is a red vegetable.

beau, bow　A *beau* is a male suitor. He may or may not *bow* (rhymes with *how* and means bend at the waist) or wear a *bow* (rhymes with *hoe*) tie, as he stands in the *bow (how)* of his boat.

beech　See *beach.*

beet　See *beat.*

being as, being that　Do not use in the sense of *since* or *because*.

berry, bury　A *berry* is a pulpy edible fruit of small size. To *bury* is to deposit beneath the ground.

berth, birth　A *berth* is a place to sleep on a ship or train. *Birth* is the process of being born.

beside, besides　*Beside* is a preposition meaning at the side of or next to: *She stood beside the car. Besides* is a preposition meaning *in addition to* or an adverb meaning the same: *Four men came besides John. He was rich, and he was handsome besides.*

between　See *among.*

bimonthly, semimonthly　*Bimonthly* means once every two months. *Semimonthly* means twice in one month, at equal intervals. The two terms should not be confused or interchanged.

　　Biweekly and *semiweekly* make a similar distinction.

birth　See *berth.*

bizarre　See *bazaar.*

blew, blue　*Blew* is the past tense of *blow. Blue* is the color of the summer sky.

bloc, block　A *bloc* is a combination of men or nations with a common interest. A *block* is a chunk of some substance, usually with several smooth sides. To *block* is to obstruct.

blue See *blew.*

boar, bore A *boar* is a male pig, sometimes dangerous. A *bore* is a dull person, usually not dangerous but always irritating.

boarder, border A *boarder* is one who takes his meals at a boarding house. A *border* is either a decorative edge or the boundary between two areas.

Boer, boor The *Boers* fought a war with the English in South Africa at the turn of the century. *Boors* are inconsiderate, rude, often loud persons. No doubt some of the Boers were boors.

border See *boarder.*

bore See *boar.*

born, borne To be given birth is to be *born.* To be carried is to be *borne: I was borne into the city by four men.* Both forms are past participles of *bear.*

borough, burro, burrow A *borough* is a political subdivision. A *burro* is a donkey. To *burrow* is to dig.

borrow, lend To *borrow* is to accept money or something else with the intention of returning it. To *lend* is to provide money or something else to a borrower with the hope of getting it back.

both Means two and only two.

bough, bow The *bough* (rhymes with *how*) of a tree may *bow* (rhymes with *how*) under too much weight. See *beau.*

bought, boughten The first is correct, the second incorrect.

bow See *bough.*

boy, buoy A *boy* may tie his boat to a *buoy,* a float anchored to the bottom of a body of water.

brake, break If one's car has faulty *brakes,* he may *break* his neck.

breach, breech A *breach* is a break, as in a wall. A *breech* is the rear part of a gun. But *breeches* are trousers.

break See *brake.*

breath, breathe When we *breathe,* we inhale and exhale air. The air is *breath.*

breech See *breach.*

bridal, bridle *Bridal* has to do with brides. *Bridle* has to do with horses.

Britain, Briton *Britain* is a short form for Great Britain, which is inhabited by *Britons.*

broach, brooch To *broach* is to introduce to the conversation: *He broached* *the subject of taxes.* A *brooch* is a piece of jewelry usually pinned to a bodice. The two words are pronounced the same (rhyme with *coach*).

buoy   See *boy.*

burn, burn up, down   Anything completely consumed by a fire is either burned up or burned down. *Up* and *down* are simply intensives here.

burro, burrow   See *borough.*

burst   *Burst* has the same form for present, past, and past participle. *Busted* is incorrect as a part of the verb *burst.*

bury   See *berry.*

bust   A *bust* is a sculpture of the head and shoulders, but not a form of the verb *to burst.*

May also mean bosom: *She had an ample bust.*

See *burst.*

cache, cash   A *cache* is either a hiding place or what is hidden in it, perhaps *cash.*

calendar, calender   We keep track of dates on a *calendar.* A machine which makes paper smooth and glossy is a *calender.*

callous, callus   *Callous* is an adjective: *A callous person is hardened in sensibility.* A *callus* is hard, thickened skin, as on a hand or heel.

Calvary, cavalry   *Calvary* is the place where Christ was crucified. *Cavalry* is mounted soldiers.

*can barely, hardly, scarcely   *Barely, hardly,* and *scarcely* have the effect of negatives. Hence, *I can barely move this morning,* not *I can't barely move this morning.*

*can, may   *Can* means to have the ability to do something. *May* means to have permission to do something: *John can run a mile in four minutes. Mary may go to the party if she wishes.*

can not, cannot   Variant forms, both correct. The latter is the more frequent.

canvas, canvass   *Canvas* is a heavy cloth. A *canvass* is a survey seeking information or votes.

capital, capitol   The *capital* is the seat of government of a state or country, where the *capitol,* a building, is located. *Capital* is also wealth invested in a business. Also, *capital* letters, *capital* offense.

carat, caret   A *carat* is a measure of weight used for precious stones. A *caret* is a mark (^) used to indicate that a word has been inadvertently left out.

carefree, careless   To be *carefree* is to have no cares, no worries. To be *careless* is to exercise too little caution.

caste, cast   A *caste* is a social class. A *cast* is an impression or mold, the actors in a play, a motion in fishing, and several other things. To *cast* is to throw.

catchup, catsup, ketchup   All three designate the same spiced tomato sauce. All three are correct.

casual, causal   *Casual* means unconcerned or without obvious design. *Causal* means relating to a cause.

cavalry   See *Calvary.*

celery, salary   *Celery* is a vegetable. *Salary* is fixed pay for a week, month, or year.

cement, concrete   *Cement* is, technically speaking, the powdery limestone substance which is used with sand and gravel to make the rock-like substance called *concrete.*

censer, censor, censure   A *censer* is a container for burning incense. A *censor* views books, plays, motion pictures, etc., with the purpose of suppressing what is to his mind objectionable. To *censure* is to criticize adversely, to disapprove.

cent, scent, sent   A penny, an odor, and the past tense of *to send* respectively.

cereal, serial   We eat *cereal* for breakfast while, perhaps, listening to a *serial* on the radio.

chased, chaste   To be *chased* is to be pursued. To be *chaste* is to be pure, especially in matters of sex.

childish, childlike   Though similar in origin, these words have greatly different connotations. To be *childish* is to show objectionable and immature characteristics; to be *childlike* is to display an ingratiating simplicity and trustful innocence.

choir, quire   A *choir* is a group of singers; a *quire* is a measure of paper, usually 24 sheets.

*choose, chose   *Chose* is the past tense of *choose. Chosen*, not *choosen*, is the past participle.

chord, cord   A *chord* is a combination of musical notes played simultaneously, or a straight line intersecting a curve. A *cord* is a string.

chose   See *choose.*

cite, sight, site   To *cite* something is to quote it as authority. *Sight* is one of the senses. A *site* is a location.

cliché, click, clique   A *cliché* is a trite phrase, one too frequently used to be effective. A *click* is a slight sharp noise. A *clique* is a small, exclusive group of people: *The fraternity boys formed a clique in the dormitory.*

climactic, climatic   *Climactic* has to do with a climax; *climatic* has to do with climate.

clique See *cliché.*

clothes, cloths *Clothes* are the garments we wear. *Cloths* are pieces of fabric, such as wash cloths or dish cloths.

coarse, course *Coarse* means not fine, rough. A *course* is a part of a student's full load of studies.

collaborate, corroborate To *collaborate* is to work closely with someone. To *corroborate* is to confirm, as a statement.

coma, comma A *coma* is a state of unconsciousness. A *comma* is a mark of punctuation.

common, mutual *Common* in this sense means shared by two or more people, but not necessarily in relation to each other: *Lee and Grant had a common objective, to win the war. Mutual* means simultaneously reciprocal: *John and Allen held each other in mutual esteem.*

complected Do not use in place of *complexioned;* not *dark-complected* but *dark-complexioned.*

complement, compliment A *complement* fills out or makes something complete. Grammatically, a complement (direct object or predicate noun, for instance) completes a predication. A *compliment* is a statement of approbation or flattery. It is usually used with the verbs *to give* or *to pay: He paid me a compliment on my acting.*

comprehensible, comprehensive Anything *comprehensible* is capable of being understood. Anything *comprehensive* is widely inclusive or capable of grasping.

concrete See *cement.*

conscience, conscious The *conscience* is the inner moral voice. To be *conscious* is to be mentally aware.

contact Some people object to the use of *contact* as a verb meaning *to communicate with.* Avoid it in the most formal levels of writing.

contemptible, contemptuous To be *contemptible* is to be worthy of contempt. To be *contemptuous* is to hold someone or something in contempt.

continual, continuous *Continual* means frequently and rapidly repeated but not uninterrupted. *Continuous* means uninterrupted repetition: *Airplanes are a continual nuisance to those living near an airport. A warning signal for an air raid is a continuous blast on the fire siren.*

*contractions *Contractions—he'll, don't, we'd—*are best avoided in the more formal levels of writing. Don't worry about them in informal writing; they're natural and effective.

coral, corral A *coral* is a sea creature which deposits a hard substance, making reefs in the South Seas. A *corral* is an enclosure for horses and cows.

cord   See *chord.*

corespondent, correspondent   A *corespondent* is the third angle in the marital triangle which leads to a divorce suit. A *correspondent* is someone with whom one exchanges letters.

corral   See *coral.*

correspondent   See *corespondent.*

corroborate   See *collaborate.*

costume, custom   A *costume* is wearing apparel. A *custom* is a mode of behavior characteristic of a society or segment of it.

council, counsel   A *council* is a group of persons, an assembly. *Counsel* is advice.

course   See *coarse.*

creak, creek, crick   To *creak* is to make a raucous, high-pitched sound. A *creek* is a stream smaller than a river in the West. A *crick* is a minor muscle spasm: *a crick in the neck.*

credible, creditable, credulous   Anything *credible* is believable. Whatever is *creditable* is laudable or praiseworthy. One who is *credulous* is inclined to believe, even on slim evidence.

creek, crick   See *creak.*

currant, current   A *currant* is a berry of the gooseberry family. A *current* is a movement, as in water or electricity. *Current* events are contemporary happenings.

custom   See *costume.*

cute   Avoid this word to mean attractive, vivacious, appealing, or winsome. All babies are cute, but hardly anything else is.

cymbal, symbol   A *cymbal* is a percussion instrument in an orchestra or band. A *symbol* is anything which points to a second level of meaning.

dairy, diary   In a *dairy* are cows; in a *diary* are records of one's activities.

dear, deer   *Dear* means precious or beloved. A *deer* is an animal.

decease, disease   To be *deceased* is to be dead, perhaps as a result of a *disease,* a sickness.

deer   See *dear.*

descent, dissent   A *descent* is a progress downward. To *dissent* is to disagree.

desert, dessert   To *dē sert'* is to leave one's post or responsibility. *Dès sert'* is the last course, usually of some sweetened food, of a meal. A *děs'ert* is a waste place, often sandy and with little vegetation.

*device, devise   A *device* is a mechanical contrivance or a stratagem. To *devise* is to contrive or to invent.

diary See *dairy*.

differ from, differ with To *differ from* is to be dissimilar; to *differ with* is to disagree.

different from, than Use *different from* except in such constructions as *He is more different (odd, peculiar) than I had expected him to be.* Not *John is different than the man I remember* but *John is different from the man I remember.*

disburse, disperse To *disburse* is to pay or expend; to *disperse* is to scatter.

disease See *decease*.

disinterested, uninterested *Disinterested* means neutral, objective, unbiased; *uninterested* means indifferent, bored, inattentive.

disorganized, unorganized Anything *disorganized* has had its organization disrupted; anything *unorganized* has not been organized in the first place.

disperse See *disburse*.

disqualified, unqualified Anyone *disqualified* has had certain privileges removed for some cause; an *unqualified* person does not have the proper qualifications for some task or position.

dissent See *descent*.

do, due, due to To *do* is to perform. Anything *due* is either owing or expected *(the train is due)*. *Due to* means *owing to;* avoid *due to* as a substitute for *because of*.

double genitive Possessives made with apostrophes and with *of* phrases at the same time are standard and correct: *That coat of Harry's, that gavel of the chairman's.* Note that the construction is usually preceded by a demonstrative adjective before the noun modified: not *the car of Tom's* but *that car of Tom's*.

downward, downwards As an adjective preceding a noun, only *downward* is appropriate: *The missile followed a downward path.* As adverbs the two forms are equally correct: *He glanced downward(s)*.

draft, draught Variant spellings. *Draft* is the usual spelling for most of the many meanings of the word.

drought, drouth Variant spellings and pronounciations of the word meaning lack of rain.

drown The past and past participle are *drowned,* not *drownded*.

dual, duel *Dual* means pertaining to two. A *duel* is a contest of honor between two gentlemen. *A duel is always a dual affair*.

due, due to See *do*.

*due to the fact that Use *because,* a clear saving of 80%.

dyeing, dying   *Dyeing* is changing color by external means; *dying* is ceasing to live. *To dye, dyed, dyeing; to die, died, dying.*

eager   See *anxious.*

economic, economical   *Economic* means having to do with the management of business, finance, etc. *Economical* means thrifty, provident.

edgeways, edgewise   Equally acceptable variants.

effect   See *affect.*

egoism, egotism   In philosophy, *egoism* is the doctrine that self-interest is a valid end of chosen courses of action. Otherwise, *egoism* means the same thing as *egotism,* an inordinate attention to oneself, conceit.

either   Usually having to do with only two: *Choose either this one or that.* Should be avoided where more than two items are involved: not *I will take either of these three over here.*

emigrant, immigrant   One who migrates away from a country is an *emigrant;* one who migrates into a country is an *immigrant.* Consequently, an Irish emigrant may become an Australian immigrant.

eminent, immanent, imminent   *Eminent* means notable, distinguished. *Immanent* is in-dwelling, inherent: *God is immanent in nature. Imminent* means immediately impending, about to take place, usually said of peril or misfortune.

enthused   Avoid; too many people object to it.

entomology, etymology   *Entomology* is the study of insects; *etymology* is the study of word derivations.

envelop, envelope   To *envelop* is to put a cover around, surround. An *envelope* is the paper covering for a letter.

especial, special   These two words are the same. However, as an adjective *special* is the more common. *Especially* is the more common adverb form.

etymology   See *entomology.*

ever, every   *Ever* means always or at any time. *Every* means *each.* The words are not interchangeable.

every day, everyday   *Every day* means each day. *Everyday* means suitable for ordinary occasions: *They use their everyday silver every day of the week.*

everywhere, everywheres   The first form is correct, the second incorrect.

explicit, implicit   *Explicit* is plain, clear, direct, not hinted at but stated. *Implicit* is implied, clearly hinted at or meant but not stated; or unquestioning, as *implicit trust.*

except   See *accept.*

excess   See *access.*

exhilarate See *accelerate*.

extant, extent *Ex'tant* means existing, not destroyed. *Ex tent'* means size or degree.

faint, feint To *faint* is to lose consciousness temporarily. To *feint* is to deceive by a false move, as in boxing or basketball.

fair, fare A *fair* is a festival; *fare* is the fee paid for transportation by bus, train, plane, etc.

farther, further In dealing with actual distance, *farther* is preferable: *He lives farther from school than I do.* In dealing with conceptual matters, *further* is preferable, but either may be used: *He is further along in school than I am. Pay no further attention to him.*

faun, fawn A *faun* is a mythological creature half goat and half man. A *fawn* is a young deer. To *fawn* is to show delight or affection in the manner of a dog or to court favor by dog-like behavior.

faze, phase To *faze* is to disconcert; avoid in formal writing. A *phase* is an aspect of a matter or process.

feat, feet A *feat* is a notable deed or exploit. *Feet* is the plural of foot.

feint See *faint*.

fewer, less See *amount*.

final, finale *Final* means occurring at the end, last. A *finale* is the last number of a musical show.

finally, finely *Finally* is the adverb form of *final*. *Finely* is the adverb form of *fine*, not coarse; delicately or in a fine manner.

fine, nice Avoid *fine* as an adjective or adverb if you mean something more specific. *This is a fine day* means only that the speaker approves of it. *This is a bright, clear, brisk day* is more specific. Also avoid *nice*.

fir, fur A *fir* is a kind of pine tree. *Fur* is the soft hair on some animals.

first, last See *former*.

flair, flare A *flair* is an instinctive aptitude. A *flare* is a torch.

flammable, inflammable These words mean the same thing, capable of being easily ignited.

flare See *flair*.

flaunt, flout To *flaunt* is to display in a showy way or boastfully. To *flout* is to treat with contempt, to mock.

flea, flee A *flea* is a small bloodsucking insect. To *flee* is to run away. It is well to flee the flea.

flour, flower *Flour* makes bread; *flowers* make a bouquet.

flout See *flaunt*.

foot Usually the singular word of a measurement is used in combination adjectives: *a six-foot man, a four-inch blade, a ten-mile run.*

for, fore, four   *For* is a preposition meaning in behalf of and a coordinating conjunction implying cause and effect. The *fore* means the front, as in forehead. *Four* is the number that comes after three. In golf, call "Fore!"

forbear, forebear   To *forbear* is to refrain from doing. A *forebear* is an ancestor.

forbid, prohibit   To *forbid* is to make a statement against an action: *I forbid you to play with matches.* To *prohibit* is to forbid with legal force: *The law prohibits parking on the sidewalk. Prohibit* is the stronger term.

fore   See *for.*

forego, forgo   To *forego* is to precede (usually used in the participial adjective forms: *the foregoing incident, a foregone conclusion*). To *forgo* is to refrain from or to renounce: *I can forgo that pleasure in the interest of time.*

foreword, forward   A *foreword* is a preface. *Forward* means toward the front or near the front, a direction.

formally, formerly   *Formally* means in a formal manner; *formerly* means heretofore, at a time preceding.

*former, latter; first, last   When speaking of two items, the first is the *former,* the second the *latter.* Do not use with more than two items. Use *first* and *last* (plus any number of intervening numbers) for more than two items. *The latter of the two incidents occurred when John was twenty. The last incident in Thompson's career was scandalous.*

fort, forte   A *fort* is a fortified place, usually military; one's *forte* is one's strong point. The two words are pronounced alike.

forth, fourth   *Forth* means onward or forward; *fourth* comes after third.

forward, forwards   *Forward* is the adjective form: *The forward ranks were neat.* Both forms may be adverbs: *I am going forward(s).* See *foreword.*

foul, fowl   A *foul* is an act against the rules of a game; a *fowl* is a large bird, usually edible.

four   See *for.*

fourth   See *forth.*

fur   See *fir.*

further   See *farther.*

gait, gate   A *gait* is a manner of walking; a *gate* is a door in a fence.

gamble, gambol   To *gamble* is to play a game for stakes; to *gambol* is to frolic or frisk about.

gate   See *gait.*

get   In addition to numerous other meanings, *get* sometimes means *become,* as in *get sick* or *get married.* In such constructions it is a linking verb and should be followed by a past participle or an adjective.

gild, guild   To *gild* is to cause to become golden in color.   A *guild* is a fellowship or society.

gilt, guilt   *Gilt* is thin gold, or a substance resembling gold, coating something; *guilt* is the condition of having committed a breach of law or conduct.

*good, well   *Good* is an adjective and should never be used as an adverb: not *She sings good*. *Well* is an adverb meaning satisfactorily, in a good manner: *She sings well*. *Well* is also an adjective meaning not ill or in a state of good health: *I was sick but now I am well*. *Well* as an adjective is almost always used after the verb.

good and   Avoid as a device for intensifying a modifier: not *John was good and sick,* but *John was very sick. John was good and bad,* meaning *John was very bad,* is hopelessly ambiguous.

a good many   This phrase means simply *many,* and can usually be replaced by *many* to the advantage of a sentence.

gorilla, guerrilla   A *gorilla* is a large ape; a *guerrilla* is a member of an irregular military force.

grate, great   A *grate* is a part of a stove or furnace. *Great* is an adjective meaning either large, important, or meritorious.

gray, grey   Of these two equally acceptable forms of the name of a color, *gray* is the more frequently used in America.

great   See *grate.*

grisly, grizzly   *Grisly* means horrible to behold, ghastly; *grizzly* means gray or sprinkled with gray. A large North American bear, *ursus Horribilis,* is, according to accounts, both grizzly and grisly.

guild   See *gild.*

guilt   See *gilt.*

had better   This idiom is usual in giving advice or issuing indirect commands: *You had better go early in the morning.*

hail, hale   To *hail* is to greet or to salute; to *hale* is to compel to go along; *He was haled into court. Hale* as an adjective means sound or healthy, usually used of older people, who are also inevitably hearty. *Hail* is ice pellets from the sky.

hair, hare   *Hair* is the covering of the scalp; a *hare* is a creature much like a rabbit. Most hares have fur, not hair.

hang   When it means to execute by means of a rope and scaffold, to *hang* is a regular verb: *hang, hanged, hanged.* When it means to suspend it is irregular: *hang, hung, hung.*

hangar, hanger   A *hangar* is a garage for airplanes; a *hanger* is a device for keeping clothes neat and off the floor of the closet.

hardly   See *can barely.*

hare   See *hair.*

heal, heel   To *heal* is to make well. A *heel* is the back part of the foot.

*healthful, healthy   Whatever brings about or contributes to health is *healthful;* whoever has good health is *healthy.* Foods are healthful; people are healthy.

hear, here   To *hear* is to perceive by ear. *Here* means in this place.

height, heighth   The first form is correct, the second incorrect.

here   See *hear.*

hiccough, hiccup   Variant spellings of the same annoying affliction.

hisself   Avoid; *himself* is correct.

hoard, horde   To *hoard* is to lay away, usually with stealth, stores of food or goods. A *hoard* is the stores laid away. A *horde* is a group, mob, or crowd. A horde of frightened women might hoard butter or canned ham.

hoarse, horse   *Hoarse* means harsh or grating. A *horse* is an animal.

hoes, hose   *Hoes* are garden implements; a *hose* is a tube for conveying liquids. *Hose* are also stockings; in this meaning *hose* is plural, the singular form having disappeared.

hole, whole   A *hole* is an opening into or through something; the *whole* means all of anything. *Whole* as an adjective means entire or complete.

holy, wholly   *Holy* means hallowed, sacred; *wholly* means entirely, completely.

home   Besides being a noun, this word is an adverb: *He will go home when he is ready.*

horde   See *hoard.*

horse   See *hoarse.*

hose   See *hoes.*

human, humane   To be *human* is to have the characteristics of a man; to be *humane* is to have the most creditable characteristics of a man, to be kind, benevolent.

idle, idol, idyll   An *idle* man is inactive, lazy, or both. An *idol* is an image of some deity. An *idyll* *(idyl)* is a simple pastoral tale in prose or verse.

*if, whether   Use *if* to introduce adverbial clauses of condition: *If you drive at a normal speed, you should arrive in two hours.* Use *whether* to introduce noun clauses of condition: *I do not know whether I will go to the game.* Clauses with *if* usually precede the independent clause; those with *whether* usually follow.

illusion   See *allusion.*

immanent, imminent   See *eminent.*

immigrant   See *emigrant.*

immoral, immortal   *Immoral* means against accepted modes of behavior; *immortal* means undying or perpetually famous.

implicit See *explicit.*

*imply, infer To *imply* is to hint strongly at a point without actually stating it. To *infer* is to derive the meaning by deduction. The speaker or writer *implies;* the hearer or reader *infers.* Whether the intended inference is drawn from a given passage depends mainly upon the skill of the writer.

in back of See *back of.*

incapable, unable *Incapable* means lacking in inherent ability or qualification to do something; *unable* means a temporary inability to do something: *John was incapable of comprehending abstruse argument. When Sally was ill, she was unable to attend class.* Note: *incapable of, unable to.*

incite, insight To *incite* is to arouse to action, to urge on. An *insight* is a penetrating understanding of something.

incredible, incredulous See *credible.*

individual Avoid this word as a noun. Use *person* or *man* or the like. *Individual* is acceptable as an adjective.

indoor, indoors The first of these words is an adjective: *We have an indoor pool.* The second is an adverb: *We like to swim indoors.*

infer See *imply.*

inflammable See *flammable.*

ingenious, ingenuous *Ingenious* means clever; *ingenuous* means open or frank.

in regard to, in regards to The first is correct, the second incorrect.

inside of This phrase can usually be replaced by *inside* or *within.*

insight See *incite.*

instance, instants An *instance* is an example. *Instants* means more than one instant; an *instant* is a short period of time.

intelligent, intelligible An *intelligent* person is mentally quick and acute. *Intelligible* writing is understandable. Most intelligent people can learn to write intelligible prose.

inward, inwards *Inward* is the adjective form used before nouns: *The idea flashed upon his inward eye.* Either form is correct as an adverb: *The girl was driven inward(s) by her hostile surroundings.*

irregardless Avoid. *Regardless* is correct.

irregular verbs Noted in verb section. See p. 18.

irrelevant, irreverent *Irrelevant* means not pertinent: *The argument about taxes was irrelevant to the matter of morals. Irreverent* means without respect for what is sacred: *The irreverent behavior of the visitors in church was annoying.*

isle See *aisle.*

*its, it's, its'   *Its* is the possessive form of *it.* *It's* is the contracted form of it is. *Its'* is a nonexistent form. The confusion of *its* for *it's* and vice versa is one of the most frequent errors in writing, and should be especially avoided.

it's me/I   Say, if you like, *it's me;* write *it is I.*

just   Avoid this word as an intensive: not *That movie was just great,* but *That movie was very good.*

ketchup   See *catchup.*

key, quay   Pronounced the same. A *key* is a device for opening locks; a *quay* is a pier or dock.

kid   Avoid this word both as a noun meaning child and as a verb meaning to *make fun of* or to *deceive.*

*kind of, sort of   Avoid as adverbs. Use *rather, somewhat,* or some other appropriate term: not *He is sort of dull,* but *He is rather dull.* When used as nouns, these constructions should be preceded by singular modifiers: not *those kind of marbles,* but *that kind of marbles.*

knew, new   *Knew* is the past tense of *know. New* means not old.

knot, not   A *knot* is a kind of a tie in rope, etc. *Not* is the word we use to make negatives.

know, no   To *know* is to have awareness of. *No* means not any or the opposite of yes.

later, latter   *Later* means more late. *Latter* is usually used with *former* and means the second of two items. See *former.*

*lay, lie   *Lay* is a transitive verb meaning to put or place. *Lie* is an intransitive verb meaning to recline. The two are often confused in some forms because of their similarity in spelling.

lie	lay	lain	lying
lay	laid	laid	laying

One way to remember which word is which is this: lay-pla (y)ce, lie-recli (e)ne.

*lead, led   To *lead* is the verb of which *led* is the past tense. *Lead* (pronounced *led*) is a heavy metal: *The miner led us to his lead mine.*

lean, lien   *Lean* is thin, not fat. A *lien* is a legal claim against property.

learn, teach   To *teach* is to convey information or attitudes. To *learn* is to absorb what is taught. We teach other people, but we learn lessons: not *I learned Arthur how to do it,* but *I taught Arthur how to do it. Arthur learned how to do it.*

*leave, let   To *leave* is to go away. To *let* is to allow, to give permission. Avoid *leave* in constructions implying permission: not *I will leave you go,* but *I will let you go.*

led   See *lead.*

lend See *borrow.*

lengthways, lengthwise Equally acceptable forms.

let See *leave.*

levee, levy A *levee* is a dike or dam to prevent floods. A *levy* is collection by force or authority: *The government imposes levies in the form of taxes.*

liable, libel *Liable* means responsible for: *Mr. Thomas was liable for the injuries Mr. Edwards suffered. Libel* is defamation by the printed word.

lie See *lay.*

lie, lye A *lie* is a falsehood. *Lye* is any caustic alkali.

lien See *lean.*

lifelong, livelong *Lifelong* means continuing throughout one's entire life: *Humming at work was his lifelong habit. Livelong,* usually used with *day* and *night,* is an intensification of *long* and implies tiresomeness.

lighted, lit Equally acceptable forms as both the past and past participle of *light.*

lightening, lightning A *lightening* is a reduction in weight. *Lightning* is a bright flash of light in the sky caused by an electrical discharge.

*like Avoid *like* as a conjunction, despite the Winston jingle; use *as if* or *as though* when introducing adverbial clauses of manner: *He looked as if he knew what he was doing.* With verbs like *do,* use *as: Do as I do. Like* is correct as noun, verb, adjective, or preposition. Making it a conjunction as well is asking too much.

likely See *apt.*

liqueur, liquor A *liqueur* is an alcoholic drink, usually highly aromatic, served typically after meals. *Liquor* is any alcoholic beverage, but usually the word refers to distilled spirits, not to wine or beer.

lit See *lighted.*

livelong See *lifelong.*

loan, lone A *loan* is the act of lending or the thing lent. *Lone* is an adjective meaning solitary, without company. As a verb, to *loan* means to *lend.*

loath, loathe *Loath* means reluctant: *I am loath to undertake the job.* To *loathe* is to dislike greatly: *He loathes his job.*

lone See *loan.*

*loose, lose As an adjective, *loose* means unfastened, not attached. To *loose* means to unfasten, to cause to be freed. To *lose* means to misplace, to miss from one's possessions: *Irene hoped that she would not lose her ring.*

lots See *a lot.*

lye See *lie.*

mad   In formal writing, avoid *mad* in the meaning of *angry*.

mail, male   *Mail* is letters, etc., brought by the mailman, who is usually *male*.

main, mane   *Main* means principal or chief: *My main reason for going was economic.* A *mane* is a heavy growth of hair on the neck of a horse, lion, or other animal.

male   See *mail*.

mantel, mantle   A *mantel* is a shelf above a fireplace. A *mantle* is a sleeveless cloak.

marshal, martial   A *marshal* is a policeman: *Marshal Dillon protects Dodge City. Martial* means warlike: *Lee was an expert in martial tactics.* (Do not confuse *marital* with *martial*. Their similarity is coincidental.)

may   See *can*.

may be, maybe   *May be* is a compound verb form: *The weather may be better tomorrow. Maybe* is an adverb meaning perhaps: *Maybe the weather will be better tomorrow. May be* and *maybe* are not used in the same clause.

mean, mien   *Mean* is an adjective denoting humble or common as well as pettily malicious. It is also a verb meaning to signify or to intend. *Mien* is a noun meaning bearing or demeanor: *He was a man of imperious mien.*

meat, meet, mete   *Meat* is the flesh of animals used as food. To *meet* is to encounter. To *mete,* usually used with *out,* is to allot: *The courts mete out justice.*

medal, meddle, metal, mettle   A *medal* is a small piece of metal cast as a reward for meritorious activity of some kind: *He won a medal for dancing.* To *meddle* is to interfere: *Don't meddle in the business of others.* A *metal* is a substance, like iron or copper, with special physical and chemical qualities. *Mettle* is courage: *The battle tested his mettle.*

meet, mete   See *meat*.

mien   See *mean*.

mighty   Avoid as an intensive adverb: not *That's a mighty good steak,* but *That's a delicious steak. Mighty* is acceptable as an adjective meaning powerful.

miner, minor   A *miner* is a worker in a mine. A *minor* is a person below the legal age for voting or certain other privileges. A miner may be a minor.

moat, mote   A *moat* is a ditch full of water. A *mote* is a grain of foreign matter in the eye, a speck of dust.

moral, morale   *Mo' ral* means in accord with accepted modes of behavior.

Mo rale' means a mental state or spirit: *After the victory his morale was high.*

more than one Although logically plural, this construction usually takes a singular verb: *More than one of the rascals is coming to the door. There is more than one way to skin a cat.*

morn, mourn *Morn* is poetic for morning. To *mourn* is to grieve. Cf. *morning* and *mourning.*

most See *almost.*

mote See *moat.*

mutual See *common.*

myself Do not substitute for *I* or *me:* not *John and myself were the first ones to arrive* but *John and I were the first to arrive.*

naval, navel *Naval* means concerned with the navy. The *navel* is a depression in the abdomen where the umbilicus was attached.

Negro Should be capitalized.

new See *knew.*

nice See *fine.*

no See *know.*

not See *knot.*

nowhere, nowheres The first form is correct, the second incorrect.

number See *amount.*

*of Do not use *of* when you mean *have,* as in *I should have come earlier.* The *'ve* of certain contractions like *would've* sounds like *of* when spoken but should not be written as *of.*

off of Drop the *of: I told him to get off his horse.*

only Try to associate this word as closely as possible with the element modified. *I only ate at their house* (but I did not sleep there) is not the same as *I ate only at their house* (and nowhere else).

oral See *aural.*

ordinance, ordnance An *ordinance* is a regulation passed by a municipal government. *Ordnance* is military supplies, now chiefly weapons and ammunition, especially heavy weapons.

our See *are.*

outward, outwards *Outward* is the adjective form: *His outward appearance was calm.* Both forms are acceptable as adverbs: *The window opened outward(s).*

packed, pact *Packed* is the past and past participle of *pack.* A *pact* is an agreement.

paddle, pedal, peddle, petal A *paddle* is an implement for propelling a canoe or playing ping pong. To *paddle* is to propel a canoe or spank a child. A *pedal* is a lever activated by the foot. To *pedal* is to work a pedal, to propel oneself by the use of pedals, as on a bicycle. To *peddle* is to travel about with goods for sale. A *petal* is a part of a flower.

paid   The past tense of *pay: He paid his debts on time.*

pail, pale   A *pail* is a bucket. *Pale* means without color, not bright.

pain, pane   *Pain* is physical distress. A *pane* is a piece of glass fit into a window or door.

pair, pare, pear   A *pair* is two. To *pare* is to remove the rind or skin. A *pear* is a kind of fruit. One could pare a pair of pears.

palate, palette, pallet   The *palate* is the roof of the mouth. A *palette* is a board upon which an artist mixes his colors. A *pallet* is a bed of straw.

pale   See *pail.*

pare   See *pair.*

parish, perish   A *parish* is an ecclesiastical or political division of a larger body or unit. To *perish* is to die.

parlay, parley   To *parlay* is to bet the winnings of one horse race upon subsequent races. To *parley* is to confer, usually with an enemy, over terms of surrender or truce.

party   Except in legal documents, do not use *party* to mean *person.*

*passed, past   *Passed* is usually the past and past participle form of *pass. Past* is usually the adjective and noun form: *Within the past week I have passed him on the street twice. Mrs. Adams has a lurid past.*

pane   See *pain.*

peace, piece   *Peace* is the blessed state of tranquility, with freedom from civil disturbance, war, or family altercations. A *piece* is a portion or fragment of a whole: *I shall not have peace of mind until I give him the piece of paper I have prepared especially for him.*

peak, peek   A *peak* is the topmost point of a roof or a mountain or a business cycle, etc. To *peek* is to look without being seen.

pear   See *pair.*

pedal, peddle   See *paddle.*

peer, pier   To *peer* is to look intently. A *pier* is a jetty, a place for tying up and unloading boats and ships.

per cent, percentage   Use *per cent* with numbers, *percentage* without: *Twenty per cent is a large percentage of the total.*

perish   See *parish.*

persecute, prosecute   To *persecute* is to harass persistently, to oppress, injure, or punish for adherence to views or principles. To *prosecute* is to institute proceedings against someone in a court of law: *If you persecute your neighbors, you will be prosecuted.*

personal, personnel   *Personal* means having to do with a person, private.

Personnel, usually a mass noun used in the singular, means employees. Whenever possible, refrain from reducing people to personnel.

petal See *paddle.*

phase See *faze.*

piece See *peace.*

pier See *peer.*

plain, plane A *plain* is a broad stretch of relatively level land. A *plane* is a tool for smoothing wood, a flat surface, or an airplane.

pleas, please *Pleas* are appeals. To *please* is to give pleasure. *Please come* means *Give me pleasure by coming.*

plenty As a noun, *plenty* is acceptable. Avoid it as an adverb: *We have plenty of wood,* but not *We were plenty tired after the trip.*

P. M., p. m. See *A. M.*

pole, poll A *pole* is a long thin piece of wood or metal. A *poll* is a systematic survey or, in the plural, the place where votes are cast: *The polls close at 7 p. m.*

populace, populous The *populace* is the whole population of a particular political unit. *Populous* means full of people, heavily populated.

pore, pour To *pore,* usually with *over* or *through,* means to look intently and steadily. To *pour* is to direct a liquid or fluid from one vessel to another: *I pored over an old book on the art of pouring tea.*

pray, prey To *pray* is to meditate or to seek communication with a deity. A *prey* is a victim of an animal which means to devour it, or, figuratively, of any creature with malicious intent: *The poor are the prey of unscrupulous speculators.*

*precede, proceed To *precede* is to go before or in front of. To *proceed* is to advance, to continue going ahead: *I shall precede you as you proceed on your appointed rounds.*

precedence, precedents *Prĕcēd' ence* is priority in rank or time: *A general takes precedence over a colonel. Prĕ' cĕdĕnts* are decisions or actions that act as models for later decisions or actions: *His election set precedents which lasted many years.*

predominant, predominate *Predominant* means superior in position or influence. To *predominate* is to prevail or to have mastery.

*prejudice, prejudiced *Prejudice* is unreasoned prejudgment. *Prejudiced* means having a prejudice, a bias. Because they sound much the same, the first is often mistakenly used for the second.

*preposition at the end of clause or sentence If doing so will result in a more natural sentence or clause than any alternatives would, end a sentence or clause with a preposition: *Sometimes a preposition is a good word to end a sentence with.* Often it isn't.

presence, presents *Presence* means being at a particular place. *Presents* are gifts.

pretty Acceptable though overused as an adjective: *She is a pretty girl.* Incorrect and overused as an adverb: *John was pretty tired after the hike.*

prey See *pray.*

*principal, principle A *principal* is the chief administrative officer of a school. A *principle* is a basic doctrine or point of a code of behavior: *I follow the principle of respecting every man's privacy.* As an adjective, *principal* means chief: *My principal interest is girls.*

proceed See *precede.*

prohibit See *forbid.*

prophecy, prophesy To *prophesy* is to forecast what is to come. The *prophecy* is what is forecast.

prosecute See *persecute.*

prove The past tense is *proved,* the past participle *proved* or *proven.* With *have, proved* is the usual form, without *have, proven: I think I have proved my point. Aspirin is a proven remedy for headaches.*

quantity, number See *amount.*

quay See *key.*

quiet, quite *Quiet* means without motion or silent, not noisy. *Quite* means either wholly (*quite dead*) or to a great degree, very (*quite near*).

quire See *choir.*

quite See *quiet.*

rain, reign, rein *Rain* is water from clouds. A *reign* is the tenure of a monarch. A *rein* is a leather strap on a bridle.

raise, raze To *raise* is to cause to rise, to build; to *raze* is to tear down. One must raise a building before he can raze it.

*raise, rise To *raise* is to lift, to cause to rise; to *rise* is to get up, to move upward, to reach a higher level. *Raise* is transitive, *rise* intransitive.

rap, wrap To *rap* is to make a sharp noise; to *wrap* is to enclose as in a package.

*real, really *Real* is an adjective: *I like real fruit juices better than artificial ones. Really* is an adverb: *John is really angry now about the election.*

Do not use *real* for really: not *That is a real good shovel* but *That is a really good shovel.*

Avoid overuse of either word.

*reason is because Avoid *reason is because* constructions. Use *the reason* *is that* instead. Or avoid the difficulty altogether: not *The reason I went there is because* . . . but *I went there because* . . .

reign, rein See *rain.*

renown *Renown* means fame, and is spelled without a *k;* it has nothing to do with the word *known.*

respectable, respectful, respective *Respectable* means worthy of respect or esteem. *Respectful* means full of respect or esteem, showing respect. *Respective* means each to its own: *The ladies went to their respective homes. Respective* can usually be omitted to the profit of the sentence.

right Avoid *right* as an adverb preceding an adjective: not *Priscilla was right glad to see me* but *Priscilla was very glad to see me.*

right, rite, write *Right* means correct. A *rite* is a ceremony. To *write* is to record speech by conventional symbols.

ring, wring To *ring* is to cause to sound, as by striking a bell. To *wring* is to compress by twisting, as in squeezing wet clothes. *Ring, rang, rung; wring, wrung, wrung.*

rise See *raise.*

rite See *right.*

road, rode A *road* is a smooth pathway for vehicles. *Rode* is the past tense of *ride.*

role, roll A *role* is a part one takes, as in a play. A *roll* is a small loaf of bread or the action of turning over and over.

round See *around.*

rout, route To *rout* is to defeat utterly. A *route* is a course of travel: *I took the shortest route to Cincinnati.*

sail, sale A *sail* is a piece of fabric to catch the wind to propel a boat. A *sale* is an offering of goods at reduced prices.

salary See *celery.*

sale See *sail.*

scarcely See *can barely.*

scene, seen A *scene* is anything viewed: *The grisly scene horrified me. Seen* is the past participle of *see.*

scent See *cent.*

sea, see The *sea* is the ocean. To *see* is to perceive by way of the eyes.

seen See *scene.*

seasons Do not capitalize the seasons: not *Spring,* but *spring.*

seldom ever Omit the *ever; seldom* alone will do the job.

semimonthly See *bimonthly.*

sense, since *Sense* is intelligence: *Jeremy has always had good sense. Since* is a preposition meaning coming after and up until now: *I have not* had a cigarette since Thursday. *Since* is also a subordinating conjunction: *Since you will not do it, I suppose I will have to do it myself.*

sensory, sensual, sensuous   *Sensory* means pertaining to sensation: *One who hears and sees well has good sensory perception. Sensuous* means pertaining to the senses in contrast to the intellect, and has a neutral or favorable connotation: *The sensuous poetry of Keats delights many people. Sensual* also means pertaining to the senses, but has the connotation of *sexual: There was no end to his sensual excesses.*

sent   See *cent.*

sentence modifiers   Some adverbs modify the ideas in sentences, not just words within sentences. For instance, *I am happily married* means one thing and *Happily, I am married* means another. *Happily* modifies one word in the first sentence, the whole idea of the sentence in the second sentence. Sentence modifiers are set off by commas.

serf, surf   A *serf* is a slave, usually Russian. *Surf* is sea waves high enough to break over.

serge, surge   *Serge* is a kind of fabric. A *surge* is a sudden swell.

serial   See *cereal.*

series   The word has the same form in the singular and plural.

***set, sit**   To *set* is to place or put, and takes a direct object: *Peter set the milk on the table.* To *sit* is to rest upon the haunches, usually upon a chair or other device; to *sit* in this sense does not take a direct object: *I often sit at my desk for hours. The figurine sits on the shelf.*

shall, will   To save untold agony, use these words interchangeably as auxiliaries in making future tenses. Usually in speaking you will reduce them to *'ll* anyway: *I'll be seeing you.* See *contractions.*

shear, sheer   To *shear* is to cut. *Sheer* means very thin, as in women's hose.

shine   As an intransitive verb, the past and past participle are *shone: The tiger's eyes shone brightly in the darkness.* As a transitive verb, the past and past participle are *shined: The police have shined their flashlights into every dark door on Skid Row.*

shone, shown   *Shone* is the past and past participle of *shine; shown* is the past participle of *show: show, showed, shown.*

shudder, shutter   To *shudder* is to tremble violently, to shake. A *shutter* is a movable cover for a window.

sideways, sidewise   These forms are equally acceptable.

sight   See *cite.*

since   See *sense.*

site   See *cite.*

slay, sleigh   To *slay* is to kill. A *sleigh* is a conveyance with runners to slip over ice and snow.

sleight, slight *Sleight* means dexterity, now usually in the phrase *sleight of hand. Slight* means slim or insignificant: *a slight boy, a slight chance.*

slow, slowly The adjective form is *slow: Audrey was a slow swimmer.* The adverb forms are *slow* and *slowly: Audrey swam slow(ly).* The first form is often used with the imperative mood: *Drive slow.*

*so Avoid as an intensive adverb: not *Edwin was so brave* but *Edwin was remarkably brave. So* is acceptable in constructions continuing with *that: Edwin was so brave that we all applauded.*

sole, soul *Sole* means *only: He is the sole heir.* The *soul* is our immortal part.

somewhere, somewheres The first form is correct, the second incorrect.

sort of See *kind of.*

soul See *sole.*

special See *especial.*

split infinitive If splitting an infinitive results in a better phrase than leaving it unsplit would, don't hesitate: split. However, if you insert too much between *to* and the rest of the infinitive you may seriously confuse the sentence: *I want to officially and very cordially, my friends, welcome you to New Haven* is somewhat abusing the splitting privilege. If in doubt, don't.

spoonfuls A *spoonful* is a measurement; more than one is *spoonfuls.* Several spoons, all full, would be spoons full. *Teaspoonfuls, tablespoonfuls, cupfuls* are also measurements.

staid, stayed *Staid* means sedate. *Stayed* is the past and past participle of *stay.*

stake, steak A *stake* is a peg driven into the ground. A *steak* is an expensive cut of meat.

stationary, stationery *Stationary* means fixed, not moving. *Stationery* is writing paper.

statue, stature, statute A *statue* is a likeness of a person sculptured in stone, wood, or metal. *Stature* means height (of persons). A *statute* is a law enacted by a legislature.

stayed See *staid.*

steak See *stake.*

steal, steel To *steal* is to take without permission something that belongs to someone else. *Steel* is a metal alloy made mostly of iron.

straight, strait *Straight* means not crooked. A *strait* is a narrow passage between two large bodies of water. A restraining device used with violent persons is a *strait jacket.* Anyone excessively strict in morals is *strait-laced.*

succour, sucker *Succour* is aid. A *sucker* is a gullible person; one is born every minute. Avoid both the word and the person.

*such a Do not use *such a* as an intensive: not *We had such a good time* but *We had a very good time. Such a* is acceptable in constructions continuing with *that: We had such a good time that we decided to stay.*

*such as Usually preceded by a comma, *such as* should not be followed by any punctuation: *Malcolm knew several exotic languages, such as Swahili, Kurdish, Tagalog, and Old Norse.*

sucker See *succour.*

suite, sweet A *suite* is a set, as of furniture. It rhymes with *sweet,* which means having the taste of sugar.

*supposed to Do not forget the *d:* not *suppose to* but *supposed to.*

*sure, surely *Sure* is an adjective: *His hand on the tiller was sure and strong. Surely* is an adverb, most frequently used as an intensifier for an adjective: *His hand was surely strong on the tiller.*

Avoid *sure* as an adverb: not *Marjorie was sure mad.*

surf See *serf.*

surge See *serge.*

suspect, suspicion *Suspect* is a verb: *I suspect him of foul play. Suspicion* is a noun: *He is under suspicion.*

swell Avoid as either adverb or adjective: not *It was a swell party.* As a verb meaning to increase in size, the past is *swelled,* the past participle either *swelled* or *swollen. Swelled* is preferred with *have, swollen* otherwise: *After my hand had swelled, it was almost as large as my swollen foot.*

sweet See *suite.*

symbol See *cymbal.*

tail, tale A *tail* is an appendage at the rear of something; a *tale* is a story.

taught, taut *Taught* is the past and past participle of *teach. Taut* means tightly drawn, not slack.

teach See *learn.*

team, teem A *team* is a number of persons associated together to accomplish something or to play a game. To *teem* is to be prolific: *teeming multitudes.*

tear, tear, tier A *tear* (rhymes with *fear*) is a drop of salty liquid produced by a special gland in the eye. To *tear* (rhymes with *hair*) is to pull apart. The past is *tore,* the past participle *torn.* A *tier* (rhymes with *fear*) is a rank or row: *The graduates stood in tiers in the auditorium.*

*than, then *Than* is a conjunction, *then* an adverb of time: *I am taller than he. Then I was foolish, but now I am wise.* Do not confuse the two because they sound much alike.

that there, this here Omit *there* and *here*. *That* and *this* are sufficient by themselves.

the See *a*.

*their, there, they're *Their* is the personal pronoun in the possessive form, meaning belonging to them. *There* is an adverb of place. *They're* is a contraction for *they are: They're taking their used cartons over there. There* is the expletive: *There is a red house on the corner.*

theirselves Avoid; *themselves* is correct.

them, those Do not use *them* as an adjective: not *Them boys are naughty* but *Those boys are naughty.*

then See *than*.

there, they're See *their*.

this here See *that there*.

those See *them*.

though See *although*.

threw, through *Threw* is the past tense of *throw*. *Through* is a preposition meaning in one end and out the other.

throne, thrown A *throne* is a chair of state, a monarch's seat. *Thrown* is the past participle of *throw*.

through See *threw*.

tier See *tear*.

till, until These words are equally acceptable. Avoid *'til*.

*to, too *To* is the preposition: *I went to town. Too* is an adverb meaning either *more than enough* or *also: Xavier was too old for the job, too.*

together with See *and*.

tortuous, torturous *Tortuous* means twisting: *a tortuous road. Torturous* means inflicting extreme pain: *He underwent a torturous experience in a POW camp.*

toward, towards These words are equally acceptable.

track, tract A *track* is a set of parallel rails for a train to move on. A *tract* is an area, now frequently a real estate development in which all houses are built at the same time from the same or similar plans.

trustee, trusty A *trustee* is a person holding property in trust individually or as a member of a board. A *trusty* is a prisoner who is given special privileges in the belief that he is trustworthy.

unable See *incapable*.

uninterested See *disinterested*.

unorganized See *disorganized*.

unqualified See *disqualified*.

until See *till*.

upward, upwards *Upward* is the adjective form: *Business was on an* *upward swing.* Both are equally acceptable as adverbs: *The man looked upward(s).*

*used to   Don't forget the *d* on *used:* not *I use to go early* but *I used to go early.*

vain, vane, vein   *Vain* means having undue pride in oneself, conceited. A *vane* is a contrivance that shows wind direction. A *vein* is a blood vessel.

vary, very   To *vary* is to change form, size, position, etc. *Very* is an intensifier meaning to a large extent, in a high degree. Avoid the too frequent use of *very.*

vein   See *vain.*

venal, venial   *Venal* means mercenary, open to corruption. *Venial* means excusable, usually used with *sin,* in contrast to *mortal sin.*

very   See *vary.*

vial, vile, viol   A *vial* is a small container for liquids. *Vile* is nasty, odious. A *viol* is any of several stringed instruments played with a bow.

vice, vise   *Vice* is wickedness. A *vise* is a tool for grasping materials, usually with a screw arrangement for applying pressure.

vile, viol   See *vial.*

vocation   See *avocation.*

waist, waste   The *waist* is the midsection of the human body. *Waste* is garbage, sewage, and the like.

waive, wave   To *waive* is to relinquish voluntarily. To *wave* is to flutter: *The flag waves in the breeze.*

wander, wonder   To *wander* is to move about, without aim, to ramble. To *wonder* is to have doubts about, to question in the mind.

war, wore   *War* is hell. *Wore* is the past tense of *wear.*

ware, wear   *Ware* means, collectively, goods, used mostly in compounds or in the plural: *The seller of hardware asked if he could taste my wares.* To *wear* is to don, as a garment: *I wear a sweater in cold weather.*

warn, worn   To *warn* is to put on guard. *Worn* is the past participle of *wear.*

wave   See *waive.*

way, weigh   A *way* is a means: *Elspeth will find a way to do the job.* To *weigh* is to ascertain the weight of.

wear   See *ware.*

wear, where   To *wear* is a verb (see *ware*). *Where* is a subordinating conjunction: *I know a bank where the wild thyme grows.*

*weather, whether   *Weather* is temporary climatic conditions. *Whether* is the conjunction introducing alternatives: *Jill meant to go to the top of the hill whether the weather was good or not.* See *if.*

weigh   See *way*.

well   See *good*.

*****when and where clauses after to be**   Avoid *when* and *where* clauses after the linking verb *to be* when a noun construction is needed: not *A hole is when you dig out all the dirt* but *A hole is an opening into or through anything*.

where   See *wear*.

whether   See *weather*.

*****who, whom**   When in doubt, use *who*. Avoid doubt by analyzing the construction in question and using *who* when a subjective case is needed, *whom* when an objective case is needed.   (See p. 30.)

whole   See *hole*.

wholly   See *holy*.

*****who's, whose**   *Who's* means *who is*. *Whose* is the possessive form of *who*: *Whose hat is on the floor? Who's to say without picking it up?*

will   See *shall*.

wonder   See *wander*.

wore   See *war*.

worn   See *warn*.

would have with **if**   Avoid *would have* in clauses introduced by *if:* not *If you would have told me, I would have gone* but *If you had told me, I would have gone.*

wrap   See *rap*.

wring   See *ring*.

write   See *right*.

yoke, yolk   A *yoke* is a part of the harness used with oxen. A *yolk* is the yellow part of an egg.

you   Avoid *you* as a generalizing device: not *When you get old enough, you can vote* but *When a citizen gets old enough, he can vote.*

*****your, you're**   *Your* is the possessive form of *you*. *You're* means *you are: Your chances are good if you're a good student in mathematics.*

APPENDIX A
HOW TO USE A DICTIONARY

We often say that we consult "the" dictionary for authoritative information on language matters. Actually, what we should say is that we consult "a" dictionary, for there are many dictionaries, old and new, good and bad, which are available. No one of them is "the" definitive dictionary of our language.

Certainly no one of them, not even the large unabridged work, is entirely comprehensive and entirely accurate when it comes off the press, and would be less than that within a week even if it were, because language constantly changes. Even a good dictionary is a good deal less than perfect.

A dictionary at its worst is an irresponsible echo of what earlier dictionaries have said, and is of less than no use because it presents as accurate and up to date what in fact is not. A dictionary at its best is an accurate reflection of the state of the language at the time the dictionary was compiled, a record of the way we use words in speaking and writing, but still not a complete or completely reliable guide to all language use.

In view of this situation, to what extent is a dictionary an authority on language? Must we accept the idea that if a dictionary says it, it's right, correct, linguistically moral? To the extent that a dictionary reflects accurately the language facts of its time and place it is authoritative, but this does not mean that it dictates how language *must* be used. It has no status as sacred writ. Anyone may use words in any way he likes. However, if a writer or speaker expects to be understood outside the narrow social circle which knows his language peculiarities, he had better use the language common to the greatest number of people, the language as it is recorded in a good dictionary. Thus a dictionary, while not an absolute authority, is a most useful guide.

Since no two dictionaries are entirely alike, one must familiarize himself with his own particular dictionary if he means to get the most out of it. Any dictionary worth owning will have a section devoted to how to use it, from which the user may find what the dictionary contains, where the information may be found, and what the various abbreviations and symbols used in it mean. *Webster's New Collegiate Dictionary,* 7th ed., for instance, prefaces the section Explanatory Notes with these words (p. 7A): "A careful reading of these explanatory notes will make it easier for the user of this dictionary to comprehend the information contained at each entry. Here are brief explanations of the different typefaces, different labels, significant punctuation, symbols, and other conventions by which a dictionary can achieve compactness."

Dictionaries usually contain two general kinds of information, *encyclopedic* and *lexical*. Although the first is not of primary importance, it is often useful. It consists of such matters as biographical information and geographical information, both sometimes in separate sections in the dictionary, sometimes not; lists of colleges and universities in the United States and Canada; abbreviations; arbitrary signs and symbols; tables of weights and measures; glossary of rhyming words; lists of given names; spelling rules; rules for punctuation; and various other kinds of information. The amount, kind, and arrangement of this material vary from dictionary to dictionary.

The lexical information is of course of primary importance. This is the information to be found in the word entries themselves. It usually includes capitalization, spelling, accentuation, syllabication, pronounciation, and derivation of the word; grammatical information like parts of speech, irregular past participles, or irregular plurals; various definitions; usage labels indicating special restrictions; synonyms; cross-references; and sometimes other matters like illustrations. The amount, kind, and arrangement of the information vary from dictionary to dictionary.

Because the content and arrangement and systems of abbreviation vary so much in various dictionaries, a user must always examine the dictionary at hand to be sure that he knows how to get the information he is after. Even the best dictionary is only as good as its user.

Some standard reliable collegiate dictionaries suitable for all but the most specialized uses are the following:

American College Dictionary, Random House
Standard College Dicitionary, Harcourt, Brace and World
Webster's New World Dictionary, World Publishing Company
Webster's Seventh New Collegiate Dictionary, G. & C. Merriam Company

The writer should acquire the most recent edition.

A couple of references for further information about dictionaries and how to use them are the following:

Adler, Mortimer. "How to Read a Dictionary." *The Saturday Review of Literature,* December 13, 1941. (Frequently reprinted.)

Mathews, Mitford M. "An Introduction to the Dictionary." A pamphlet issued by the World Publishing Company and available free.

APPENDIX B
A SELECT LIST OF USEFUL BOOKS

History and nature of language:

Laird, Charlton. *The Miracle of Language.* New York: Fawcett World Library, 1960. An inexpensive reprint of the eminently readable 1953 volume on the origin, nature, and development of language.

Baugh, Albert C. *A History of the English Language,* 2nd ed. New York: Appleton-Century-Crofts, Inc., 1957. A standard college text on the development of the English language.

Grammar:

Brown, Dona Worrall, Wallace C. Brown, and Dudley Bailey. *Form in Modern English.* New York: Oxford University Press, 1958. A lively exposition of sentence patterns and grammatical signals.

Conlin, David A. *Grammar for Written English.* Boston: Houghton Mifflin Company, 1961. A recent successful attempt to blend the traditional and linguistic viewpoints on grammar.

Usage:

Bryant, Margaret M., ed. *Current American Usage.* New York: Funk and Wagnalls, 1962. Limited in coverage but authoritative.

Evans, Bergen, and Cornelia Evans. *A Dictionary of Contemporary American Usage.* New York: Random House, Inc., 1957. The most comprehensive work available.

Nicholson, Margaret. *A Dictionary of American-English Usage.* New York: Oxford University Press, 1957. A revision of Fowler's justly famous work on English usage, brought up to date and adapted for Americans.

Rhetoric:

Graves, Harold F., and Bernard S. Oldsey. *From Fact to Judgment,* 2nd ed. New York: The Macmillan Company, 1963.

Johnson, James W. *Logic and Rhetoric.* New York: The Macmillan Company, 1962. Explanations of rhetorical principles and patterns of organization, with many examples.

General:

Perrin, Porter G. *Writer's Guide and Index to English,* 3rd ed. Chicago: Scott, Foresman and Company, 1959. A most useful guide to composition, grammar, mechanics, and usage.

APPENDIX C
WORDS FREQUENTLY MISSPELLED

(See Glossary of Usage for some of these words which are misspelled through confusion with similar words.)

accept
accidentally
accommodate
accompany
accomplish
accustom
achieve
acquaint
acquire
across
actually
adolescent
affect
against
all right
amateur
among
amount
analyze
apparent
appearance
appreciate
approach
approximate
argument
arouse
article
athlete
attack
attendance
attitude
authority

before
beginning
believe
benefit
boundary
Britain
business

capital
careful
carrying
category
certain
challenge
character
chief
choose
chose
clothes
coming
comparative
condemn
conscience
conscientious
conscious
considerably
consistent
continuous
controlled
controversy
convenience
council
counsel
counselor
criticize
curiosity
curious
curriculum

dealt
decision
definite
dependent
description
desire
despair
desperate
disappoint

discipline
disease
divide
divine
dominant

effect
efficient
embarrass
entertain
environment
equipment
especially
exaggerate
excellent
excitable
exercise
expense
experience
explanation
extremely

fallacy
familiar
fantasy
fascinate
favorite
fictitious
field
finally
financier
foreign
forty
forward
fourth
friend
fulfill
fundamental

government
grammar

guaranteed
guiding

happiness
height
heroes
hindrance
huge
humorous
hungry
hypocrisy

ignorance
imaginary
immediately
incidentally
independent
indispensable
influential
intellect
intelligent
interest
interference
interpretation
interrupt
involve
irrelevant
its
it's

judgment

knowledge

laboratory
laborer
laid
led
leisure
length
license
likelihood

117

= sentence
8 parts of speech (Comma
11-43   48
— Common Errors
55-65

livelihood	performance	relative	suspense
loneliness	permanent	relieve	symbol
loose	permit	religion	synonymous
lose	persistent	remember	
luxury	personnel	reminiscence	technique
	persuade	repetition	temperament
magazine	pertain	represent	than
magnificent	phase	response	their
maintenance	philosophy	rhythm	themselves
maneuver	physical	ridiculous	then
marriage	piece		theories
mathematics	planned	sacrifice	there
meant	playwright	safety	therefore
mechanical	pleasant	satire	thorough
medicine	politician	satisfied	those
medieval	possess	scene	thought
mere	possible	schedule	to
miniature	practical	seize	together
mischief	precede	sense	too
mischievous	predominant	sentence	tragedy
morale	preferred	separate	transferred
	prejudice	sergeant	tremendous
narrative	prepare	several	tries
naturally	prevalent	shepherd	two
necessary	primitive	shining	
Negroes	principal	significance	undoubtedly
ninety	principle	simple	unnecessary
noble	privilege	sophomore	unusual
noticeable	probably	source	
	procedure	sponsor	vacuum
obstacle	proceed	stories	various
occasion	professor	straight	view
occurrence	prominent	strength	villain
omit	propaganda	strict	
operate	psychology	studying	weather
opinion	pursue	substantial	weird
opponent		subtle	where
opportunity	quantity	succeed	whether
optimism	quiet	success	whole
original		summary	whose
	realize	supposed	women
paid	receive	suppress	writing
parallel	recommend	surprised	
particular	referring		yield
perceive			you're

An enlightening article on spelling is Pollock, Thomas Clark, "Spelling Report." *College English,* XVI (October, 1954), 102-109.

A useful book devoted to the problems of spelling is Shaw, Harry, *Spell It Right!* New York: Barnes and Noble, 1961.

INDEX